D1569652

Frank Augustyn

Dancing from the Heart:

A MEMOIR

Frank Augustyn

M&S

WITH BARBARA SEARS

Canadian Cataloguing in Publication Data

Augustyn, Frank, 1953-
  Dancing from the heart: a memoir

ISBN 0-7710-0875-9

1. Augustyn, Frank, 1953- . 2. National Ballet of Canada – Biography. 3. Ballet dancers – Canada – Biography. I. Sears, Barbara. II. Title.

GV1785.A93A3 2000   792.8'092   C00-931483-0

Every effort has been made to assign credit for photographs. Reported errors will be corrected in any reprint.

We acknowledge the financial support of the Government of Canada through the Book Publishing Industry Development Program for our publishing activities. We further acknowledge the support of the Canada Council for the Arts and the Ontario Arts Council for our publishing program.

Book design by Kong Njo
Typesetting by Cathy Deak
Typeset in Centaur by M&S, Toronto
Printed and bound in Canada

McClelland & Stewart Ltd.
The Canadian Publishers
481 University Avenue
Toronto, Ontario
M5G 2E9
www.mcclelland.com

1 2 3 4 5   04 03 02 01 00

To Erene, Kyra, and Nicholas

CONTENTS

PROLOGUE

The walk from the Mayflower Hotel to the Metropolitan Opera was a very familiar one. I had done it many times before. I pass the dry cleaner's, the empty lot, the apartment buildings, a small café and restaurant, and, at Broadway, the Ballet Bookshop. Then, in the distance, there it is: the glorious and intimidating Met. The grand fountain and the Chagalls are inspirational, but on performance days they seem more like visions an artist must conquer. This would be my first performance of the New York season with the National Ballet of Canada, and before New York first nights the feelings were always the same: a sense of anticipation and excitement accompanied by crushing, almost overwhelming, anxiety. In fact, whether it was the Met or any other theatre in the world, the journey to the dressing room for me was always an exercise in self-control. Once I got into the theatre, the anxiety level would drop a little, although it would never really go away until I took my first steps.

There was one way, though, in which this journey was unlike all the others I had made before. The performance this evening would tell how much I had — or hadn't — matured as an artist. It was 1988, and although I did not know it, I was near the end of my career as a classical dancer. The ballet was John Cranko's *Onegin*, and I was to play the title role. It was a difficult role for me, one which depended more on interpretative ability than physicality. I had studied it intensely, perhaps even overstudied it. Onegin was a tortured and lost soul, and I needed to draw on more dramatic skill here than I ever had as a prince. In addition, the pas de deux in *Onegin* are among the most difficult John Cranko had ever choreographed, and he was never easy at the best of times. I had prepared the role for over a year, and had performed it in Toronto. Now, all the preparation was to get its final test, in front of a New York audience that I knew could kill me. I was partnering the National Ballet's rising star, Sabina Allemann, who had more than proved herself in the equally demanding role of Tatiana.

That night, Sabina and I were lucky — the performance gods smiled on us, and we were as near flawless as I can remember. At the end, the audience stood applauding, loudly enough that I am sure they could hear it all the way back home in Hamilton. I felt, at that moment in the Met, that I had truly arrived as a mature artist. It had taken me eighteen long years.

Frank Augustyn

Steeltown Beginnings

Hamilton, Ontario, in the 1960s was not known as a cradle of dance stars, and ballet was not an art form my family knew much about. We were a fairly typical working-class family of four, my mother and father, my older brother, Peter, and I. My father, Wladyslaw, had come to Canada from Poland shortly after the war, in 1948, and had settled in Hamilton, which was then, as now, a blue-collar town of steel mills and factories. After several different odd jobs in construction, he went to work on steel-plate welding at the Stelco plant, a job at which he remained for most of his working life.

My father had artistic talent. He was an excellent painter, and that is probably what he should have been, but earning a living was his prime concern, and he knew he couldn't do that as an artist. He had to make money to bring my mother, Elizabeth, over to Canada from Germany,

With my brother, Peter, left. An early performance.

and to support the family. Painting for him remained a passion all his life, but he never saw it as a living. This attitude of his to the arts would colour his whole approach to my career.

Walter — which was how his name was anglicized — was one of eight children, a farm boy born in the country near Warsaw. Physically a small boy, he was lost in a large family of five brothers and two sisters, always feeling he had to fight for whatever he could get. From the very beginning, my father was a scrapper, and in later years, many of his most famous scraps would be with me. At the age of sixteen, he contracted rheumatic fever, which weakened his heart. He remembers lying in bed watching his chest heaving up and down, his heart racing. Each morning, his father would come into the room to check up on him. "Is he dead yet?" he would ask one of his other sons, fully expecting that he would be. My father, fighter that he already was, determined that it would take more than a bad heart to get the best of him.

His main goal in life was to be in the army, which for him was a way out of farm life. His relatives tried to discourage him from joining up, because of his health, but once he had recovered from his illness, my father refused to believe there was anything wrong with him. He managed to convince the army that he was military material, even though he was only five foot five and had a bad heart. That says something about how short of recruits the Polish army was during the Second World War, but it didn't stop my father being very proud of the achievement. Throughout his life, he retained an admiration and respect for military people.

During the war, he was captured twice, the first time by the Russians. He escaped from a Russian prison camp, arriving home weak, malnourished, and weighing under ninety pounds. At first his own mother didn't recognize him. She nursed him back to health, but soon afterwards the German military took over Poland. He was taken prisoner and sent by train to the Black Forest region of Germany, where he was forced to work on a farm managed by Catholic monks.

Later, he worked in a wheat mill, where he was supposed to wear the letter "P," to indicate he was a worker from Poland.

After the war, he settled in Schramberg, Germany, studying at a technical school for Polish refugees. It was here that he first met my mother. My father had rented a room in a house across the road from the apartment she shared with her father. She was twenty-three years old, a beautiful girl, with striking, long copper hair. She had lived in the small Black Forest town all her life and, at the time they met, she was working in an office. They saw each other for about a year, before my father set out for Canada in 1949, settling with one of his brothers in Hamilton. For over a year, my mother and father wrote to each other. Then, in 1950, he sent her the money to come out to Canada. Shortly after that, they were married. They had both come to start a new life with little more than the clothes on their backs.

For the first two years of their married life they lived with my father's brother, Stanley. In 1952 they bought a tiny house with only three small rooms on Robins Avenue in Hamilton. It was very inexpensive, as my father did not like the idea of a mortgage. Never buy anything you can't pay for, he was fond of saying. He never wanted to owe anything to anyone. All they owned when they moved in was my brother Peter's baby carriage. Every last penny they had managed to scrape together had gone into the house. At first, they sat on boxes in the kitchen and slept on the floor. Later, somebody gave them a chesterfield and chairs, which my mother still has today. Only gradually did they fill the house with other furniture.

I was born in 1953, and during the years of my childhood, my brother, Peter, was my best friend. He was one year older than me, but we did everything together. We went to the same school and the same dance class, and when it came time to get a part-time job, we shared it. I was eight and he was nine, and with our canvas bags emblazoned with *Hamilton Spectator* we delivered newspapers to sixty-five houses on Tragina Avenue after school, for which we earned the princely sum of $3.50 each a week. The first time I ever felt any sense of mission was delivering this paper. That was the day of the Kennedy assassination in 1963. I didn't know who Kennedy was, but I knew whatever had happened was important, as people were waiting at the door for the newspaper. I felt important, too. After all, I was the one bringing them the big news.

Throughout our childhood, Peter was the sensible one. I was more reckless. Peter would have to rescue me when I raced my bike downhill, careening off into a ditch and knocking myself out. He was the one who abided by our father's dictum: save. Not me. I always wanted to rush out to spend the money we earned on the paper route. Although we were great friends, it was clear to me even then that Peter and I were very different people. Years later, Dawn Vale, our grade-school teacher, would accurately describe the differences between us: Peter, she said, was governed by duty; Frank, by ambition. I was almost alone amongst all the grade-schoolers she taught who had an idea at a very young age of what they wanted. I went, she said, in my own direction, without any regard for where anyone else might be headed.

My father wasn't around much during my childhood. There were times when we wouldn't see him for days. Often, when he was on the eleven-to-seven night shift at Stelco, he would be sleeping when we got home from school. To make up for this absence, and to help us know who he was, my father felt that it was his responsibility to tell us about his life. But he didn't just talk to us, he would lecture. On Sundays, he would call us into the front room, and we would be expected to sit there and listen. The stories were always the same: about the war, the farm in Poland, his friends and the things they got up to, which seemed to consist mainly of hunting, fishing, and causing a lot of trouble. There were lots of stories about the fights he got into. If they were all true, he was getting into fights at least once a week.

These lectures became an inescapable fixture in our lives. After five or six minutes of fidgeting and being irritated, I would accept the fact that I had to sit and listen to him, and would settle down. Once he got started, the stories were actually very interesting, although I can't say that I got the moral of them all. My father liked to listen to himself talk, and he thought that by telling these stories he would command our respect. He desperately wanted us to admire and respect him. It was a rather strange and awkward way of striving for this, but I do know that he cared tremendously for us. My father was really proud of having sons. There was a not-so-friendly competition between him and my Uncle Stanley, his older brother, who had four daughters. In Eastern European homes, as in a lot of cultures, having girls was okay, but having sons was what really mattered, so Uncle Stanley was on the losing end here. My mother later told me that Stanley had to take nerve pills to get through visits with my father.

My mother, Elizabeth, was far more of a presence in our lives. She was the one who took care of us, doing the cleaning, the cooking, making sure we were set for school, helping us with our homework. The warmth in our home came from her. I found it was easy talking to her about my innermost feelings, something I could never imagine doing with my father. My mother has a great sense of humour, and my brother and I would enjoy teasing her. At times, we'd go too far and she'd let us know. She'd get angry and chase us around the house with a ladle in her hand, and we'd run to the bathroom, because it was the only room in our house with a door you could lock.

I am sure my parents loved each other, but our family home was not a peaceful one. It seemed to me that they fought most of the time. When they were together, any form of decision-making could become a fight. It made me feel ill, as it would anyone, to see two people I loved fighting. Like all children, I wanted my parents to be friends, to be happy together, and absorb me and my brother into their happiness. Even a simple thing like deciding where to go for the Sunday walk could provoke a huge fight. On one occasion, my father wanted to go one way, my mother another, and, as they could not agree, I went with my mother, and Peter went with my father. Suddenly, going for a walk

Above: A family portrait, taken when I was four.

Below: My favourite acrobatic tricks (show off!)

 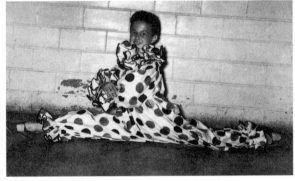

wasn't fun any more. I wasn't with Peter, and it was painful to me that the family could not do something so simple without fighting. At night, Peter and I would lie awake in the double bed we shared and listen to the fights. Sometimes, I would try to break it up. I'd yell at them to stop arguing, but even if they stopped and the smoke cleared, I'd still be unable to sleep. I hated the fighting, and most of the time I tried not to think about it. I was pretty good at that – pushing things away, trying to bury them – but it wasn't always possible.

Acrobatic classes were one avenue of escape. Even when I was very small I loved running and jumping. I was such an energetic child that my mother thought I might like acrobatics. An advertisement in the *Hamilton Spectator* announced Eileen Lee Morrison's classes in a studio only a few blocks away from our house in northeast Hamilton, so Peter and I decided to try it out. The dingy basement studio didn't put either of us off. I was soon enrolled and instantly obsessed. I loved doing aerial cartwheels, handstands, front and back flips. Soon I was good enough for Eileen and her daughter, June, to suggest that I enter a Kiwanis competition for acrobatic dance. That was where ballet came in. To help me with acrobatics, they offered free ballet lessons, which they thought would build my strength. Reluctantly, I agreed to give ballet a try.

The first ballet class I took, I hated. In acrobatics, I'd been used to running, jumping, and throwing my body around. In ballet, the first thing I had to do was stand still, like a mannequin. Then I had to hold onto this piece of wood which they called a barre, and slowly point my feet. Front, side, back, then back, side, and front again. It was slow, precise, and I was bored out of my mind. I absolutely hated it. Only pressure from Eileen and June made me continue. Grimly, I fixed on the idea that I had to do this because it would make me a better acrobat. In theory, it may have done so, but when it came to competition time, I froze. Everything that I could do so perfectly in practice went out of my head on stage. My mother and the rest of the audience watched a floundering, embarrassed ten-year-old improvise badly. Needless to say, I didn't win first prize. I didn't do many competitions, but when I did, I usually got second or third. Only once did I win a competition. That time it was expected. I was, after all, dancing with my teacher's granddaughter, Harriet Henry.

Queen Mary Public School was my second avenue of escape. It was a tough place – not an ideal escape, perhaps, but interesting for all that. It had gangs, a lot of fighting, and characters like Dennis Davies. Dennis Davies – tooth knocked out, black eyes, black buzz-cut hair with a cowlick, a real tough guy. The tooth that had been knocked out was replaced by a silver cap, so that when he smiled, he had one shiny, silver tooth. It made him look even meaner, like a pirate. I tried to give Dennis a wide berth. With characters like him, the school playground often seemed more like a battlefield, with opposing gangs staking out territory and challenging each other to fight.

Queen Mary had about a thousand students, most of them from working-class families. They were solid, hard-working people, but it was the kind of place where nobody asked questions when a student didn't show up at school – that usually meant the rent hadn't been paid for a couple of months, and the family had skipped town. At Queen Mary, my favourite classes were music and history. Dawn Vale, my grade-five teacher, has an abiding memory of me walking on my hands around the classroom, then refusing to take the hint when she said "Thank you, Frank. That's enough."

Throughout my years at Queen Mary, school and dance class were two separate worlds. I lived a sort of Dr. Jekyll–and–Mr. Hyde existence. I had my school friends and I had my dance and acrobatic classes at Eileen and June's dance academy. I didn't say anything about dance class to anyone at school. This wasn't deliberate; I assumed that after school all kids did other things, like playing hockey. Dance was just what I did. It never occurred to me to tell the other kids I danced, though, looking back at it now, I can imagine what the likes of

Dennis Davies might have said, had they known. At the time, I had no conscious idea that there was any stigma attached to boys dancing, but somewhere, somehow, I must have known that it would not have been a good idea to publicize my activities too much along the back streets of Hamilton. Any reservations I had must have been slight, though, because they were definitely not serious enough to stop me appearing on *Tiny Talent Time*, broadcasting my interest to the world.

That was a highlight for me. *Tiny Talent Time*, produced at CHCH in Hamilton, was something of an institution back then, and I was delighted to be chosen to go on the program. Bill Lawrence, now the weather man on the CBC, hosted the show, which consisted of young children showing off their performing talents in their chosen fields. It was all incredibly folksy then, as it still is, but children and parents alike loved it. I performed in what would then have been called a Red Indian outfit – green felt loincloth with fringes, sewn together by my mother and handpainted by my brother with an eagle and a sun. To match the outfit, Peter painted a sun on my chest and a red eagle on my back. What else could the routine be called but "Hiawatha"? It was done to a simple drumbeat, and consisted mostly of acrobatics.

Before the show, I was sitting in Bill Lawrence's office waiting to go on, shivering with cold, so he put his sheepskin coat over my shoulders to help keep me warm. All I could think was that his beautiful coat would be spoiled with a red-eagle image all over the white sheepskin. I sat rigid, not wanting to lean back and get his coat messed up. The performance, before an audience of doting relatives, went well. Everybody applauded at the right times, and for me, it was all very exciting. I loved the performing part of it, but it was also exciting to be on TV with Bill Lawrence, who we thought of as a big star. After the taping, we all went home and watched the whole program again on television.

Despite the "performing flea" in me, I was a shy child with a tendency to daydream. I lived in my own little world, and could be oblivious to what was going on around me. There were times when this could cause me and those around me a measure of grief. After school one day, I arrived home to find that no one was there. More than that, there was no furniture in the house – it was completely empty. I went outside onto the verandah to check the house number, and yes, I was in the right place. I ran back inside and upstairs. The house was totally empty. I remembered finding a nickel a long time ago, and hiding it behind the television set in the living room. I looked and, yes, there was my nickel, where I had placed it, still on the floor, so I had to be in the right house. Then I remembered my parents talking about buying another house on the same street. I couldn't remember in which direction, but I knew it was somewhere on this street. I thought, they've moved, but didn't tell me. Why didn't they tell me? I went outside and, after running a block, I saw a truck. There, of course, were my mother and my brother. But it was very traumatic, because I thought, for those few moments, that I had been abandoned. I thought I must have done something really bad for them to leave me. My mother swore up and down, saying, "Well, we've been talking about this for days!" Then she realized I was really upset, and went and bought me a chocolate bar to smooth things over.

Although it was only a block or so along the street, our new house was bigger than the old one, with two bedrooms upstairs. It was also more solid, built of brick. We had moved up a notch in the neighbour-hood, a fact that did not please our new Anglo-Saxon neighbours. They didn't like us – we were immigrants, after all – and they showed it. "Go back to where you came from," one of them once spat at my father. For thirteen years, we lived in a house beside people who refused to talk to us.

I had not been taking ballet class for long when my teachers, Eileen and June, recognized I had talent. One day in 1963, they spoke very seriously to my mother, saying they should have experts look at me, and I was sent for a week to a summer school run by the National Ballet. That was when the National Ballet School principal, Betty

Oliphant, first saw me. "I have to have that boy," she said, and promptly set out to get me. She called my parents and offered me a place at the school. That was how we found ourselves, my mother, father, and me, on the bus to Toronto, all dressed in our Sunday best, on our way to check out the National Ballet School.

The school had been running for only a few years, but already it was the place to study in Canada if you wanted to be a classical dancer. Betty Oliphant and her colleague Celia Franca, who was then artistic director of the National Ballet Company, had set up the school with the intention of grooming dancers for the company. The standards for admission were exacting for girls, a little less so for boys, but I didn't know that at the time.

On arrival, I was put into a class. I felt out of place. "Why did I agree to do this?" I thought. "I should have stayed home."

After the class, we went into Betty Oliphant's office. This was my first meeting with a woman who would be instrumental in shaping my early education as a dancer. Betty Oliphant was single-minded in her dedication to the school. She had built it from the beginning, and ran it with total authority. To a child of ten, she seemed a kind woman, with a warm smile, and I felt comfortable with her. She was, of course, doing everything she could to get me into the school, and it was only later that I found that Betty was far more complicated than she seemed to me that day. "Would you like to dance one day?" she asked. "Yes, I would," I said, which was not exactly the truth. I wasn't at all sure I wanted to dance. "You're very talented," she added. From the very start, she said that I was good, and that I could, one day, if I wanted to, be a "top-notch dancer." That gave me confidence; it was uplifting. Betty then added: "Boys are rare in ballet." This appealed to me. I was interested in anything that was unique or out of the ordinary. I didn't stop to question why boys were rare in ballet.

Betty told my parents about the school facilities. I would receive my academic education, as well as my ballet education, and at the end I

would have a high-school diploma. Betty believed firmly in the importance of dancers getting a good academic education. At that time, it was
very expensive to go to the National Ballet School, and when she said
what it was going to cost – $2,500 a year – my father intervened.

"There's no way," he said. "We don't have that kind of money.
We can't afford that."

"How about if you pay half?"

"No," my father said. "If you want him, you're going to have to
somehow find a way, because we can't."

Betty was resourceful and she did find a way. I eventually got a full
scholarship for the whole time I was at the National Ballet School.

However, my parents wouldn't let me attend right away, as they
thought that, at the tender age of ten, I wasn't old enough to leave
home. They were firm with Betty that I stay at home until I was
twelve. My father wasn't keen on my attending, anyway, and I wasn't
at all sure that I wanted to go either. Ballet was still just something I
did because it would help my acrobatics. I only kept at it because I got
a great deal of support and encouragement from my teachers.

This semi-committed attitude to ballet changed dramatically when
I was twelve. That was when my mother took me to the Palace Theatre
in Hamilton, where the National Ballet was performing *La Sylphide*. I'd
never been to a theatre before. I was fascinated by the people milling
around, the red plush seats, the warmth of the place, and the subdued
lighting. Down in the pit, the orchestra was playing something that I,
knowing nothing about warming up, thought very ugly. Then the lights
dimmed, the curtain rose, the dancers came on stage, and I was
transfixed. A magical world opened up, in which the movement of the
dancers spoke directly to me, instantly drawing me into their story and
their feelings. I did not know it then, but I was watching one of the few
traditional ballets where both the drama and the dancing centre on the
hero. Right up there, on stage, was something I knew I wanted. I wanted
to be that hero. I thought, if that's what ballet is, if that's what ballet will

let me be, then I'll stand at that barre, and I'll turn my legs out in that awkward way, and I'll point my feet. I'm twelve years old, I thought. I'd like to play like this for the rest of my life. Instead of running away to the circus, I was going to run away with the ballet company.

The following day, I looked at the *Hamilton Spectator*, and there in the arts section was a photograph of the very same people I had seen perform, Earl Kraul, Lawrence Adams, Lois Smith, and Celia Franca. The women were in cocktail dresses and the men were in suits and ties. Looking at this photograph, I suddenly realized these people *were not children*. They were as old as my parents. I had thought they were kids dressed up. Seeing the dancers out of their costumes, in regular clothing, looking like my parents, was a shock. Then I thought, if old people can do this, I will be able to dance forever. Betty Oliphant had said I could be a dancer. Now, after watching *La Sylphide*, I actually wanted to be one. That one performance planted a powerful new idea in my head. A few months later, I saw Margot Fonteyn and Rudolf Nureyev on the *Ed Sullivan Show*. Now I was really hooked. I bought a thirty-nine-cent photograph of Nureyev at Coles in the Centre Mall in Hamilton, and pinned it on my bedroom wall. Acrobatics receded into the distance as I concentrated on turning myself into a ballet dancer.

As the time approached for me to take up my place at the National Ballet School, my father still had serious doubts. In the end, he let me go, thinking that, if I went to the ballet school, then, when I graduated at seventeen, I would smarten up, go to college or university, and get a real job. He was, I think, proud of the fact that I was to attend a private school, but he was also tormented by my uncle's reaction to the prospect of my going away. "You're a fool," my uncle said. "You've sold him. You've sold your son." My uncle thought that sending a child away to boarding school at the age of twelve was a heartless thing to do. My father had to deal with that. Only later did I realize that he also had to deal with telling his friends at the Stelco plant that his son was going to ballet school.

CHAPTER

2

The Education of a Prince

I set out for the National Ballet School in September 1965, full of nervous excitement. I was going as a full-time boarder, although I knew I could come home to Hamilton on weekends if I wanted to. The morning of departure, I got up at five o'clock, said goodbye to my father and brother at home, and my mother took me to the bus terminal in Hamilton. I watched my mother waving on the platform as my bus pulled away. The bus had to turn the corner, and by that time she had followed it, and stood watching and waving again. I had a lump in my throat. I had never been away from my parents before, and I was homesick before I had even left. "It's not as though you're leaving for the rest of your life," I said to myself. But it felt that way. Maybe the feeling wasn't that far off the mark, for the

With Wendy Reiser, in the main National Ballet School studio,
a converted Quaker church.

world I was entering was a long way from the smokestacks of working-class Hamilton.

The main school building was located on Maitland Street in downtown Toronto, with our residences and some smaller classrooms around the corner, on Jarvis Street. Both academic and dance classes were held mostly at Maitland Street, in a converted Quaker church, which was where the main school studio was located. Much of my time over the next five years would be spent in this studio. For me, this room, more than any other, evokes the essence of the school. It is a serene place – a light, airy studio with high windows letting in shafts of sunlight, a room of graceful proportions, with warm wood floors. In this room, my body would grow and change, slowly re-shaping its form into that of a classical dancer.

At first, I was the only boy in my class. There were other boys in the school, but they were all older than me. Modelled on the Royal Ballet School in London, the National Ballet School was a boarding school of some ninety students, mostly from wealthy or middle-class families. I was now amongst children whose families were far better off than mine, but, during all the time I was there, I was never made to feel inferior. If there was a ranking at the school, I soon found out that the ranking came from talent, and I felt okay about that. Talent was something that Betty Oliphant had assured me I had.

I had to get used to boarding school: to sharing a room with three other boys, wearing a uniform, and eating school food, which was pretty dreadful – meat patties with over-boiled vegetables, the typical residence food of those years. I also had to get used to long days of hard physical and mental work, and to being away from home five days a week. Not only did we cover the Ontario high-school academic curriculum, we also had many dance classes. We got up and breakfasted, and at eight-thirty the working day began. Two academic classes, then ballet class. Then lunch, which lasted

twenty minutes or half an hour. Then another type of class, modern
dance, based on the Martha Graham technique, or eurythymics, or
theatre arts, or character class, or yoga. Then two more academic
subjects. Then another dance class, such as a partnering class. Then
dinner. Then the boys would go to Jarvis Collegiate to do gymnas-
tics. This was primarily for developing the upper body, and at the
end of the session we'd have fifteen minutes to kick a ball around.
We'd get back to residence at about eight-thirty, have a snack, do
homework, go to bed exhausted. Then the whole round would start
again at eight-thirty the next morning. It didn't help that I was
an insomniac.

I simply endured the academic side of school – the math, history,
geography, science, and languages. A memorable low point was
getting 22 per cent in math. I cared, but not much. After all, it wasn't
what I was there for. My math teacher once asked me to stand up and
look at a problem on the board. She explained the system to me over
and over and over again, and didn't want to let me go until I got the
right answer. The trouble was, I couldn't get the right answer because
I still didn't understand it. At that point, she came over to my desk.
Normally, she wasn't one to yell, but this time, she did. She pounded
her fist on my desk – in frustration more than anger – crying "Frank,
Frank, Frank." I sat there feeling so badly *for her*. I was sure it wasn't
because I didn't have a talent for math; I was just not interested. I
knew what two plus two was, and I knew how to buy something.
What more, I thought, did I need?

One academic teacher who made some impression on me was
my French teacher, Mrs. Lucy Potts. She spoke English, Russian,
German, and French fluently, and was a hugely talented teacher. With
a glint in her eye, she recognized I had a sense of humour, and she
always seemed to know what I was thinking. It wasn't that I was good
at French, but she kept trying, with this very knowing eye and patient
way. I never did especially well in French in school, but when I left

Above: An academic class, with a group of attentive students. Karen is at left.

Below left: The boys' residence — a group of friends. Robert Desrosiers is front centre.

Below right: Our masterpiece in the art room.

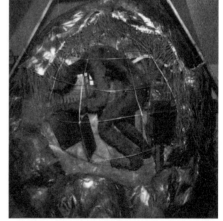

school and I had to work with dancers whose first or second language was French, I found I could communicate. Not well, but at least I could communicate. Somehow the words Lucy Potts had fed me came back when needed.

I struggled through the academics only to get to what really mattered to me, which was the dance classes. In my first years at the school, my dance teachers were women, mostly Jeanie Geddes and Betty Oliphant. Jeanie taught the younger children in the approved style, which was largely a carbon copy of Betty's way. She was a pleasant, amusing woman, and a good teacher. But the school was Betty's baby. Betty was the one we all wanted to impress.

Betty was honest to a fault. You always knew where you stood with her, but sometimes she would hit you between the eyes with her honesty – in a way that wasn't always appropriate and certainly wasn't always kind, at least in the short term. I soon found out that many of the students were afraid of Betty, but I never feared her. In fact I quite enjoyed her, partly for the understandable reason that I was getting enormous encouragement from her. If *she* thinks I'm good, then I must be good, I thought. I also liked her because we could talk, and because we had the same sense of humour. But Betty's sense of humour was only one aspect of her personality. She was also an extremely exacting taskmaster. Betty was really hard on us, which I thought was fine; she should be hard on the students.

I was the only boy in a class of about sixteen girls, which I soon found out meant that I got special treatment. She gave corrections and sometimes was pretty severe – maybe even mean – to some of the girls. On one occasion she made this girl cry. "I don't understand," she said. "You all cry and cry. I've made all of you cry. And look at Frank. Whenever I scream and yell at him, he just smiles or laughs and gets on with it. Why can't you be more like Frank?" She didn't get it, she just didn't understand how severe she was with the girls. What she said about me was true, though. Whenever she bawled me out, I

Betty Oliphant corrects Wendy Reiser.

would smile at her and try to do it correctly. But I wouldn't cry, and I wouldn't get upset.

Years later, when I interviewed her for the television series *Footnotes*, I asked her if she preferred teaching boys to girls. She said, "Oh, yes, absolutely. Boys are a heck of a lot of fun. With boys, they always told you what they felt, they were always very honest with you, as I was with them. With girls, you never knew." She added, though, that boys were also more difficult to teach than girls, a sentiment echoed by other teachers. I also talked to the director of the Paris Opéra Ballet school, Claude Bessy, about this. She said the same thing, adding that, with boys, for years you think you are getting nowhere. Girls progress. You can see it every month, they're getting better, they're listening, learning, they're attentive, and *very* serious. Boys, on the other hand, don't care much – or at least, you think they don't. They don't seem to listen, they slop around. They don't improve, and they like to laugh a lot. Then suddenly, you don't know what happened, but they excel, just like that, with no warning. And no one knows where it comes from. Girls progress steadily; boys tend to explode at one moment in their lives.

In the upper years, our main teacher was Daniel Seillier, who came from the Paris Opéra Ballet, where he had been an excellent character dancer. He was very important to me, because he was my first male dance teacher, and I was able to identify with him at a time when I badly needed male role-models. He was a very hard man, and in many ways I think he had Short Man's Syndrome. Daniel was only about four foot nine, and we all towered over him. As we grew, it just got worse. Daniel had many good qualities as a teacher – he could move fast, he had great strength, and he was a good actor; but he was demanding. It was Daniel who taught me discipline. He pushed us very, very hard and, because he was so small and could move very quickly, the tempi in the exercises he gave us would require us to move fast. We were gangly and growing into our bodies, and struggling to do things which he executed with no problem at all. It was from Daniel that I got my speed and my strength. I also learned from him how to do one step at a time. Do it very, very well, and only then move on.

Daniel Seillier practised a finely tuned art of intimidation. I saw him hit people. I saw him take a lighted cigarette and place it under a student's leg so that she or he would hold the leg up à la seconde. Linda Maybarduk, one of the students in a class above me, complained one day that her foot was sore and she couldn't do the class. Daniel got really upset, yelling and screaming – all in French, of course, because he refused to speak English. He emphasized that, in order to be a dancer, you have to be able to endure pain, and he took a darning needle that the girls used to darn the tips of their shoes, and he pinched the skin on his arm. He then took the needle and put it through the fold of skin. All this to demonstrate to Linda what it meant to withstand pain. She almost fainted watching him and the rumour promptly went around the school that not only had he pierced his own arm, he had pierced her arm, too. On another occasion, he went up to my friend Robert Desrosiers and slapped him across the face because Robert wasn't doing the exercise properly. Robert, who has a temper himself, slapped Daniel right back across the face, yelled at him, and stormed out.

Despite all this, I got along well with Daniel Seillier, although there were times when he could have been a little more tactful. I remember in one of my report cards he recommended that I wear contact lenses, because, when I took my glasses off to dance, I looked as if I couldn't see. So, the following year, my parents did invest in a pair of contact lenses for me. On the next report card, Daniel wrote, "It's great that Frank has his contact lenses, but unfortunately he still looks as if he can't see."

Daniel and Betty did not always get along, and certainly did not always agree on how a child should be taught. They fought so much that people would ask why she didn't get rid of him. She never did, because she wanted him there – not just because he was a good teacher, but because, I think, she enjoyed being challenged. She could be a little perverse that way. Betty enjoyed a fight, perhaps because she felt it kept her sharp. Take the mirrors in the studio. Betty didn't believe in mirrors in the studio. Daniel did, since he came from the Paris Opéra, where there were plenty of mirrors around, and where they were used as an integral part of teaching. When I first arrived at the school, there was only a single tall mirror in the big studio, and if you needed to see yourself, then you had to go to the corner of the room to look. It was an old mirror, covered in little black marks, and was fading fast. No one liked to use it. Daniel felt that mirrors were essential for dancers to use to correct themselves. In the end he went out and bought mirrors for the studio with his own money and had them installed. Betty believed a dancer should feel rather than see positions. There was, she said, no mirror there to guide you in a performance. So she turned around and paid for drapes to go over Daniel's mirrors. That way, Daniel gave classes with the mirrors, and Betty closed the drapes and gave her classes without them.

Both their classes were very intense, as was everything at the school. The peer pressure, the hormonal explosion, and on top of all this, the academics made for a potent mix. Ballet schools have been described as boot camps, and there is a measure of truth in this. I think there was a sense of breaking down the students, in order to build them again in a certain mould. There was always a "you are not as good as you think you are" attitude. In addition, we were constantly told "you're only as good as your last class." In other words, there was no let-up whatsoever. It was a matter of first learn the craft, then prove yourself again and again, and then, maybe, your dancing will gain approval. This was tough, but that was why I loved it. I liked the people in the school, and the fact that so many of them were also interested in dance. I liked the fact that we danced, all the time. We danced in residence, we danced at dinner, we danced down the street, we danced in the studios, we danced before our academic classes began. When we weren't dancing, we enjoyed talking about movement and dance and exercises and techniques. Like all students, we spent a lot of time complaining, too. About our teachers, and our principal, and the residence food.

What we were being given was a gift: an instrument with which to create. That instrument could not exist without discipline. Many dancers who have been at the school, then have gone on to other things – modern, jazz, or tap, or singing – complain that its method is stilted and without freedom of expression. My response is that, if there's no expression, it's because the person did not allow their own expressiveness to come through. It has nothing to do with the teaching or the art form. It's like saying that a great violinist is stifled because they're getting all the notes right. Many dancers have said to me, "How could you stand that place? You have to be so precise and perfect." There was venom coming out of them. In fact, a lot of people who have graduated from the National Ballet School hate it with a passion. Many feel they were mistreated by the school, saying they were exposed to a kind of psychological torture, and to be fair, Betty Oliphant was only interested in the really good dancers, so if you weren't really good, you suffered. The girls also suffered if they were putting on too much weight. They were promptly told to lose it, and were ignored until they did. In addition, if a child in the process of growing lost the something special that had got them into the school in the first place, Betty would just lose interest. In many ways, it was an unforgiving place, and definitely was not for everyone, but I was lucky. I got the attention I needed and I loved it.

My first year at school, when I was twelve, I was chosen to dance in *The Nutcracker*. That was wonderful, because it gave me a chance to see the company's life. I was able to touch my future. If I had had my way, I would have beamed myself up at that point into the National Ballet of Canada, as a fully fledged, completely educated dancer. I didn't want to go through all the boring work that was necessary to get there. Here were principal dancers Lawrence Adams, Earl Kraul, and Lois Smith, whom I had seen in *La Sylphide*, and, of course, here was Celia Franca, who was directing the company. With her striking physical appearance and air of total authority, she seemed little short of God to me. Right from the beginning, I was intimidated; I could see she kept everyone in order by instilling fear. Celia was a master of the embarrassing insult, and kept everyone on edge, as we never knew what she was going to say. Rehearsing *The Nutcracker* one day, she turned to a girl in the company who wasn't doing the right steps, and said, "What is it, dear? Do you have a headache? Is it that time of the month, darling?" The girl broke into tears and ran out of the studio. Celia, like Betty, showed nothing but impatience with such displays of sensitivity.

I had very small parts in *The Nutcracker* — a child, one of the courtiers, and a clown. At the very first rehearsal, after I had learned the *Nutcracker* steps in the studio, I was in a line-up of boys on stage left. There was a line-up of girls on stage right, and we were to march towards each other, taking twelve or sixteen steps, starting with the right leg. We all started marching with the note, and I started marching with the wrong leg. Celia stopped the music and said, "Frank, you must start with your right leg." I was terrified. The music started up and, again, I started with my left leg. "No, Frank, no, no, no!" Celia yelled. I was twelve years old, publicly taken to task in front of my peers — and my heroes. We started again, and, once again, I started marching with the left leg. By now, I was in a state of shock. This was the first time I had had professional dancers watching me. Celia stopped the music again. There was dead silence. This time, she came down from the podium, and pinched my right leg hard, until it really hurt. That way I remembered. Start marching on the leg that hurts.

It was during my second year at the National Ballet School that I ran into some trouble with kids about my age hanging round on the street. In many ways, I was still an innocent. I still saw it as completely natural for a boy to go into ballet, and at the time it never occurred to me to ask why I was the only boy in my class. I didn't know that a large number of male dancers were gay, and that, consequently, given the attitude of those days, there was a stigma attached to men in dance. I was aware that there was a stigma attached to dancers in general, as being intellectual boneheads, but I was completely unaware of the attitude that said real men don't dance. The school was situated in a rough neighbourhood and one day, on my way from residence to class, a group of street kids on bikes started teasing me, calling me names. They wouldn't let me pass. They started pushing and shoving, and I wasn't about to be pushed. I got very angry and literally took one of the bikes by the handlebars and lifted it and turned it upside-down, with the guy on it. I was in very good shape — probably a lot better shape than they were — and I was angry. When you're angry, you have more strength than you ever thought you could have. The others stepped back for a moment, I angrily put my foot into the bike spokes, and then took off.

It was an awakening. Back at school, I talked to other boys in the class about what had happened, and that's when I found out that everyone laughed at us and thought we were, in the argot of the day, faggots. This was the first time I encountered prejudice against boys and men in ballet. The images I had of men dancing were strong and I wondered how anybody could think there was anything wrong with it. It was a complete puzzle to me. It put a whole new slant on Betty Oliphant's comment "boys are rare in ballet." However, I quickly learned to stay away from situations in which I could get into trouble. The last thing I needed was an injury or a black eye or a missing tooth.

Most of my good friends at the school were boys. Robert Desrosiers, who would go on to found his own company, as well as choreograph works like *Blue Snake* for the National Ballet, was one of them. We shared a room together. One evening, we both woke up at three or four in the morning. I realized he was awake, we turned on the light and, talking, we found we had had a very similar dream. We had both dreamt of someone falling through a tunnel. There were a lot of colours attached to this. We decided to go to the art room and build our dream.

We started working on this project as soon as our art teacher, Mrs. Goss, gave us the go-ahead. We made papier mâché and bought lumber and wire, and essentially made a structure that would have filled a twelve-foot-square room. We built a man falling and swinging within a globular encasing, red inside and grey on the outside, all of papier mâché. There were lights coming up around this man, who moved through the air by the use of a fan underneath. There was a sense of light and movement within the sculpture. To support the whole thing, we built a wooden external structure. It was huge.

To get our masterpiece finished, we used to break into the school after hours on Saturdays and Sundays. Students weren't really supervised on weekends; we could do whatever we wanted. Except, that is, go into school. Fortunately, I found a way of picking the lock. Once in, Robert and I would shut ourselves into the art room and continue working. It came to a point, as the structure was being built, that we'd also go there in the evenings on weekdays. Whenever we felt we could do something, or we had some new material, we'd break into the school again. We seemed to have four hands and one brain. Robert and I thought in similar ways, but it was amazing that we should have had such a similar dream. The sense of falling, spinning, and being enclosed tells me that we both felt a bit trapped, a bit lost. Our monstrous sculpture was our way of dealing with this. When it was done, it took up more than half the art room, which meant that Mrs. Goss had very little space for her classes. She brought Betty Oliphant to the third floor of 113 Maitland Street, to see the monstrosity we had created, and Betty loved it. Then, for the next two weeks, Mrs. Goss kept begging us to get that thing out of there, because she needed her classroom, but Robert and I couldn't bring ourselves to destroy it. So she eventually destroyed it for us. One day we came to class, and it was gone.

Robert and I were always looking for adventure. On another occasion, Mrs. Goss asked us both to collect some wood for her. To do this, we needed a car. Unfortunately, neither of us really knew how to drive – and neither of us had a licence. I was still only fifteen. Mrs. Goss lived further along Maitland, and we had to take her car from her home, go up the alley behind the school, pick up the wood, come back down the alley, and deliver the wood. It was one block. "No problem," I said. Robert was equally confident as she gave us the keys.

"*Merde*, I drive my dad's truck all the time," he said, stretching the truth a little. "I drive the Jeep, I drive the tractor, don't worry about it."

"I'll drive it there, you drive it back," I suggested. Well, I drove it. I completely knocked down the fence beside the apartment building behind the school, and caused quite a lot of damage to the car. We gathered the wood, put it in the car, and Robert, who at least had *some* driving experience, drove it back. We were both shaking when we told Mrs. Goss what we had done. She was very understanding and didn't get angry with us, but we were a little more cautious about claiming we could do things after that.

Weekends, we were at loose ends, always looking for things to do. We would break out of residence at three, four, five o'clock in the morning, climb down the television aerial, and roam the streets of

Toronto in the dead of night. Up and down Yonge Street we would go, past the strip clubs and massage parlours that littered the street in those days. For kicks. It was just fun to be out and breaking the rules. There was nothing to it, since we never actually went inside any of those dens of iniquity. All we did was run around the streets, and then come back. We did it a couple of times. Then, the novelty wore off. On to something else. For me, weekends also meant breaking into the closed school to get into the library, and I'd spend hours there on my own. A tiny book-lined room, it was an oasis of calm for me, the big window letting the sun stream in as I sat curled up reading. I would devour anything on Roman history, art, architecture, and, of course, ballet.

All this breaking out and breaking in constituted very mild acts of rebellion. As I got older, I became more serious about rebellion, to the point of being a ringleader in a walk-out from the school. It was the sixties, the years of protest, and even students at the rather conservative National Ballet School could do their tiny share of protesting. What it was over escapes me now, but it had something to do with how the residence was run. It mattered enough that all the boys walked out, which would have horrified our parents — that is, if they had known. Mr. and Mrs. Boardman, who were our caregivers, sharply told us that we weren't allowed to do it, but we walked on by, ignoring them. We wound up on Isabella Street, where one of our classmates, Michael McKim, had what seemed to us dormitory boys to be a very glamorous apartment. It was very sixties, all black walls, and Michael had a squirrel monkey for a pet. When we looked around the room, we could see had deservedly earned his name of Shithead.

We phoned Betty Oliphant from Michael's apartment, to tell her where we were and what we had done. We obviously weren't quite as rebellious as we liked to think we were. Betty said that we should go back to the residence, and that we could discuss our problems in the morning. She added that we wouldn't be reprimanded, because she understood our problem was serious, and she would do everything she could to rectify it. To me that sounded reasonable. So we all trooped back to residence, and, with our matrons standing there, we walked up the stairs and into our rooms and obediently went to bed. The next day, we had a meeting with Betty Oliphant, and the problem, whatever it was, was resolved. I learned something from that incident. Not every problem needs a rebellious act to be dealt with. Betty was wise here: she showed us that she would listen to our problems, and that change could come from talking. Flexibility was always one of Betty's great strengths in running the school.

It was shortly after this that I first saw a man who would have an enormous impact on my life and my career. Rudolf Nureyev had come to Toronto with the Australian National Ballet, in his own production of *Don Quixote*. It was seven years after his 1961 defection from the Soviet Union, and he was by then the shining star of the ballet world. I knew the stagehands at the O'Keefe Centre (which is now the Hummingbird Centre), so I was able to get into the backstage area quite easily. I watched him prior to a performance, in the rehearsal space backstage, doing his barre, which was very exact and precise. He then did some centre exercises, tailored to his performance. I was mesmerized. I stood there shyly in the doorway, decked out in my NBS school uniform of green blazer, white shirt, green tie, grey slacks, and brown oxfords, as the great star of ballet swept by, paying no attention whatsoever to a lowly student looking on in awe.

He gave a great performance, very fiery, as you would expect, but it didn't all go well. In the last act, he entered upstage right, took a huge promenade to downstage, piqué into arabesque and balance, all in total silence. Then he pliéd, the music started, he did two steps and fell splat on his butt. Ballet's greatest star was flat on the ground. He stood up, the music was still going, and he did something almost unheard of – he walked off. The conductor stopped. Robert Desrosiers, who had a small part as a cup-bearer, was standing in the wings near the rosin box. Robert said Rudolf came offstage snarling, complaining about the stage, and rubbed his feet into the rosin, all the while using the robust vocabulary of swear words that I would later get to know only too well. He came back on stage, took the same long promenade in total silence, using even *more* time. He then did a wonderful variation, made better because of the fall. Most dancers just get up and continue after a slip. Rudolf had used the mistake to show the audience what he could do. I saw there for the first time a perfectionist on stage. It was clear he was giving everything. To an aspiring dancer of fifteen, he was a hero, a living legend. He gave pride and legitimacy to the role and art of men in ballet.

While at the school, I also met for the first time another great icon of twentieth-century ballet, Erik Bruhn. Like Nureyev, he also would later become an important influence on my career, but to a fifteen-year-old student he was a blond god, one Betty Oliphant had unwisely compared me to. Betty was fond of saying that I was going to be the next Erik Bruhn, and I was painfully aware that the whole school had heard this from her. Erik had come into a class Betty was teaching to observe, and I wasn't sure that he hadn't heard it, too. Erik was impassive throughout the class. I swear his face never moved; cobwebs could have grown on it. He had walked in – so I knew he was alive – but he sat there for an hour and a half and literally did not move. Betty gave me a jumping exercise to do alone, in front of the class. I hated the idea of being singled out, and could only think that he was sitting there thinking that Betty was crazy to imagine that I might be another him. It was mortifying. I finished my piece, and there was no reaction at all from Erik. This opaqueness I later learned was characteristic. It contrasted sharply with Betty, who was bubbling and enthusiastic. I felt humiliated and embarrassed. I came away with the feeling that, at the risk of

Above: Erik Bruhn, centre, with Betty Oliphant, visiting the school.

I am out of frame, to the left.

Below: Daniel Seillier taking class.

embarrassing everyone in the room, including herself, she had wanted to show how much she believed in me.

In the upper years of the school, when we were fourteen or fifteen, we began to do partnering classes. These classes were not as numerous as those for solo work, but they were a very key part of my education as a dancer. Here I learned the basics: how to work with and manipulate your partner so that she can dance as freely as possible, feeling as though she is dancing on her own, while knowing you are there to help her. I learned how to adjust and keep my partner on her balance, without losing my own. I also learned how to lift, and about the importance of using your knees – that way, you have more strength. And I learned how to guide pirouettes without digging into my partner's ribs or waist and hurting her. Above all, I learned how important it was to move together to the music. This was the fundamental common ground: working together with the music. Without it, the dancing is mechanical.

Murray Kilgour and Nancy Schwenker taught us partnering class. Murray was very good at teaching the more intangible aspects of how to be a good partner. From him, I learned the deportment of a male partner: how to look at my ballerina, how to present her, where to stand in relation to her. It really helped that Nancy and Murray not only liked each other a lot, they were falling in love. When I watched them working, I saw before me a regal and giving prince, with a princess constantly paying attention to him. It was the emotion I read between the two that fed me. What I saw in Murray and Nancy as they danced for us was so appealing. It was so wonderful to see the two working harmoniously together.

The more I progressed, and the harder the steps became, the freer I felt as a dancer. As I added more steps to my dance vocabulary, I felt I could say more with my body. By the upper level we had double tours, attitude turns, cabrioles, double assemblés in our repertoire. I

found this very challenging. I particularly enjoyed the jumping steps —
that feeling of being in the air, and stopping for a moment before
descending. It's an illusion, of course, you don't actually stop, but if
you become still for a moment at the top of a jump, you create this
illusion of a frozen moment. That's the way jumps are supposed to be
done, giving the feeling that you are lighter than air. This was a joyous
time for me — I was getting better and better, and I was happy being
told how much I was improving.

Everything went well for me until my fourth year at the school. I was
sixteen, and when I came back after the summer holidays, I had
grown. I got back into the studio and suddenly I couldn't do anything.
Anything. Even simple movements, which I had mastered years earlier,
were now beyond me. I was at a loss to understand what was going on.
In fact, it was quite simple: what had happened was that my muscles
hadn't kept up with my growing skeleton, which occurs with a lot of
children. But knowing that it happened to many children didn't make
it any easier to deal with. I felt so clumsy. All I could do was work
through a terrible and depressing year, when I worried that I had lost
my way. I couldn't do anything in ballet class, my grades were slipping,
and I was constantly tired.

This was the first time my dancing suffered, but my grades were
still terrible. I hadn't changed since the early days when my self-
assurance as a dancer had meant that I was also cocky as an academic
student. Who cared about terrible grades? I was king of the hill in
dance, and this was, after all, a dance school. I was talented, everyone
seemed to believe in me, everyone thought I could be one of the best
dancers in the world. What else did I need? Why did I need to learn
and study? If I was forced to do anything, I resented it, so stubbornness played hand-in-hand with what my teachers consistently described
as laziness. Maybe I should have worked harder academically, but it
was more difficult for me to do that than to dance. So I took the easy

road and didn't do it. An early comment from Betty Oliphant on my report card is typical: "Like most talented boys, Frank is very lazy. He has to be constantly prodded to work. The talented student produces either extraordinary or mediocre results, according to the discipline he places on himself. At the moment, Frank's teachers place the discipline. That is their duty. But in a few years' time, he will be on his own, and there will be no one to make him work. I advise him to take this to heart now, as his future depends on it." In characteristic fashion, I did not take anything to heart, and, if anything, the next report card was even worse. This time, I think they were trying to scare me into working. "Frank is always polite. In class he is inclined to daydream, and is often inattentive. He does not like to exert himself mentally. He is lazy, and must make a real effort to work in all subjects. Frank is wasting his time, and has no right to accept a bursary unless he is willing to work." Those were harsh words, but they had very little effect. The following term, my marks were worse still. Singlehandedly, throughout my years in the school, I pulled the class average down.

I could have given up and gone home any time I wanted. My parents always said, "If you don't like it, you come home any time you want." I think they half-hoped that I would. But there was never any question in my mind of my leaving the school, and even my visits home became less frequent. At first, I'd go home on weekends. Then the workload got heavier, and, gradually, my visits were reduced to every other weekend. Then the workload got heavier still, and it turned into once a month. It was just too tiring, after having two or three ballet classes on Saturday, to take the bus home, only to come back to school the next day. I was being stretched to the limit physically and emotionally. Teenage years are particularly difficult when you are a dancer.

There was more to it than that, though. My relationship with my father, which had never been particularly good, was going downhill fast. We fought constantly, over everything, particularly religion and politics. Our arguments were usually provoked in some way by the trivial events of the day, but on another level they came down to some very fundamental differences. On religion, my father was old school: he believed in a God on his throne in heaven, and in Mary, Jesus, the Catholic Church, the Pope, and the whole religious hierarchy. My view of God could not have been more different: it had nothing to do with churches and hierarchies. Simply put, I felt that God was within us all. On politics, where my father saw all politicians as acting in their own self-interest, I was far less cynical about why people did things. I really believed, and still believe, that it is possible to be motivated by the idea of doing good for humanity.

My father was so sure he was right that he was unwilling to listen to argument. If we were close at all at this time, it was in battle. Fighting my father was my connection with him – in challenging him, insulting him, questioning him, I experienced a closeness which could not be gained any other way. Peter, my brother, was appalled. He was the conciliator in the family, who got along with my father in a far more easy-going way, challenged him less, tolerating what he could not change. I, on the other hand, was determined to convert my father to my point of view. My father and I shared one thing: a fierce determination to convert each other.

My mother and I got along better. She understood that the dancing was something I really wanted to do. More than that, I think it was something she would have liked to do herself, because she was a natural performer. Through me, she saw a life that she might have liked for herself, although to her credit she never became one of those typical show-business mothers, who push their children forward at every opportunity. She left me to find my own way.

During my last two years at the school, I was hired to perform with the Canadian Opera Company for the season. I'd complete my schoolwork and be excused at the end of the day to go to opera rehearsals. We'd work evenings and weekends. It was here that my education on how the world saw the sexuality of male dancers continued. This was at a time when, though sexually interested in girls, I didn't have any experience. There were several gay opera singers who were very overtly showing an interest in me. It was all very new to me, and the approaches from gay men made me extremely uncomfortable. Once, after a performance, I got a note from one of the opera members, asking me to come to his room. I didn't go. Another time, I was in the hotel room that I shared with another dancer, but he wasn't there. There was a knock on the door. It was an opera singer from the chorus, wanting to talk to me. I invited him in, since we had chatted before at the theatre. He talked for a bit, then he started wanting to kiss and hug me, at which point I threw him out of the room.

On that particular tour, it wasn't only men that I had to learn to deal with. During one performance, a woman singer came up to me and propositioned me. She was much older, in her forties, and one of her dresses would have made three outfits for me. The proposition was very direct; there was nothing subtle about it. It hit me between the eyes — drop-your-drawers-and-let's-do-it. I thought, What's wrong with me? Is anybody else being bugged like this? The other dancers I was dancing with were older than I was, in their twenties and thirties. They were established artists, secure in themselves. I think everyone saw me as the naïve, vulnerable kid I was. At the time I found it very upsetting. All I wanted to do was get back to school and my classmates. Although I did do a second season with the opera, it was easier. By then, with a little more maturity, I had learned how to handle these situations better.

At the end of my grade-eleven year, in 1970, Betty Oliphant called me into her office. "I think you should go," she said. I was in shock; I thought she was kicking me out of the school, which, given my appalling academic record, would not have been surprising. Then she continued. "The National Ballet has one more position open, and I think you should go there." I was delighted. I was out of school a year early, at the end of grade eleven. True, there would be no high-school diploma, but I didn't care. Even though she generally believed in dancers getting their academic credentials, in my case, I think Betty saw that this was the right move. Why go through another year of bad report cards? I was lucky – I never had to go through the anguish of the big audition, as the girls all did. I had, in fact, been auditioning for the company in an informal way since I first appeared in *The Nutcracker* at age twelve. Celia Franca had watched me progress to the point at which I was now – a seventeen-year-old budding dancer.

I went home at the end of that term, triumphant. That summer, there were constant fights with my father, who thought I should come back to Hamilton, finish high school, and get a job. He was shocked when I said I wanted to join the National Ballet Company and make a career of dancing. His arguments were all sound: there was no security, you got paid very little, you'd work nine months of the year and then get laid off. What happened, he asked, when I was too old to dance? How would I earn my living then? I wasn't looking at economic reality in those days, and I certainly wasn't looking that far into the future. I was looking at something I really wanted to do – the only thing I really wanted to do. It was something I was good at, and something people were prepared to pay me to do. That, I couldn't believe: that anyone would actually *pay* me to dance. I'd be a fool to turn it down. My mother, on the other hand, understood how much the opportunity meant to me. That mattered to her. She worried less about what might eventually happen to me than my father did. Even though my father kept trying to convince me that it was a bad decision, I was determined to join the company. Finally, he suggested I try it for a year, and, if it didn't work, I could go back and do grade twelve. We left it at that, but I had absolutely no doubts I was in this forever. I wanted to be not just a corps de ballet dancer, but what Betty Oliphant had said I could be – "a top-notch dancer." I was going to be a principal dancer with the National Ballet of Canada. I was determined to prove to everyone that I could do it.

CHAPTER

3

Company Life

In the fall of 1970, I joined the National Ballet of Canada as one of its forty-one dancers. I was now taking classes alongside men I had once admired from a distance: here was Jeremy Blanton, who I knew as a wonderful partner; Hazaros "Laszlo" Surmeyan, with his intense dramatic air; and here was Clinton Rothwell – tall, cool Clinton, with his leather jacket and motorcycle. Looking around at these people, I felt I had arrived. I was a professional dancer, I kept saying to myself. I had a paycheque to prove it. True, corps de ballet pay at $3,500 a year wasn't great, and there was no job security at all, but at seventeen, job security was the furthest thing from my mind. It shouldn't have been. I soon found out that people were worried about being fired at a moment's notice, which Celia

A portrait taken shortly after I entered the company.
I was still uncomfortable posing.

41

Franca had been known to do. We all knew that if we wanted to stick around, we had to measure up to Celia's exacting standards.

Celia ruled us with an iron fist. Not many people said anything to challenge her. Of course, we never, ever, called her Celia then. It was always Miss Franca. Those were the years when ballet companies really were run from the top down. Democracy was an unheard-of concept in the National Ballet of those days. It wasn't exactly that dancers were taught not to ask questions; we just knew that asking questions of the artistic director was not something you did if you wanted to stick around. It should be said that there was a comfort in all this, because we knew exactly what our boundaries were. Celia had created a family unit, in which she was the parent, the mother figure, Miss Franca. Her dancers – *her* dancers – were the children. Grown men and women in their forties were called girls and boys. Every last one of us was struggling to please Celia. Fear of what she might say and what she might do united us all.

In many ways, the National Ballet of Canada in 1970 was Celia. She had been its director since its inception in 1951, and had developed a company that reflected her tastes and her standards. It had all the standard classical works in its repertoire, along with a smattering of new choreography. Celia chose the repertoire. She chose the dancers. She hired designers. She cast productions. She rehearsed us endlessly, until what we did met with her approval. What Celia had created by 1970 was a solid, middle-rank company that had yet to break into the first rank. The National Ballet of Canada had never played New York and it had never played London, England. When we toured, the venues were not the major opera houses but small theatres in places to which the larger, more-established companies never travelled. I did not know it at the time, but Celia had already determined to change this. She had bigger things in mind for all of us. If she was hard on us – and she was often hard on us – it was in pursuit of her goal to make the National Ballet of Canada a company of the first rank.

Celia was tough to please. I never felt that she was completely satisfied at the end of a rehearsal. There was never a sense of "yeah, finally, you're on the right track." It was a more restrained "it's getting better, darling, but . . ." There was always that "but." Once, while rehearsing a variation, I landed out of position and, in anger, hit the floor with my fist. This made Celia laugh. "Good boy," she said. "Good boy." Instead of the usual reprimand, I got praise for being angry with myself. I may not have been conforming to her standards of performance, but at least I was measuring up in behaviour, and that seemed to matter almost as much.

Celia didn't want anything rebellious or individual in the company. What she wanted was conformity to the standards she set. You had the personality and style she gave you. It was as simple as that. We willingly and enthusiastically went along with this, because, in the context of Canadian ballet at the time, Celia was the unquestioned expert. She had, after all, danced with the Sadler's Wells Royal Ballet and with the Metropolitan Ballet. She had founded the company and endured great hardships in getting it on its feet. She knew ballet. And what did we know that she hadn't taught us?

I never came under Celia's most exacting scrutiny, because I was a man, and useful because there were so few of us. Generally, Celia was a little more careful with the men, and I think she liked them better and enjoyed working with them more than with women, much like Betty Oliphant. What complicated her relationships with the women was her transition from dancer to artistic director: she wasn't dancing the big roles any more; others had to do it for her. To them, it was made very clear that there was a right way and a wrong way to do things. The right way, of course, was Celia's. It took her a long time to lose the notion that there was only one right way.

Although Celia was not as hard on me as she was on the women, she still had her moments. I soon realized I had a lot to learn, particularly as a partner. From very early on, I had been trained to do solo work, but we weren't trained as much to think of two instruments working in tandem, and here the demands on the male dancer are in some ways greater. The man has to know the woman's steps before he can even begin to partner. I was plain green. I knew the basics, about pirouettes and promenades, and some lifting, the basic technique of using your legs to lift, not your back. Beyond that, not much. I was learning on the job.

The situation wasn't helped by the fact that one of the first dancers I had to partner was extremely nervous. I wasn't sure why she was that way, whether it was because I was so young and inexperienced, or whether she was just nervous all the time. I had to work almost instinctively with her, putting more concentration into helping her than anything else. Forget calming her down – saving her was more like it. Every time she did a step for which she needed support, I saved her – if I hadn't, she would have been on the floor. It was never a complete disaster, but it could have been. It made me much more aware of what partnering means.

In *Four Temperaments*, a Balanchine work that explores the ancient idea that the human body consists of four humours, we had to do much that we had not been taught in school. We were cast in the second movement, where there is a particularly difficult move in which the woman turns on point in plié, with the partner spinning her. I thought it was neat, I'd never done it before, but I had to admit that it was hard even for someone who wasn't nervous. Our rehearsals were difficult. Stage performances were worse. She was visibly shaking. At first, I thought that maybe, if she were dancing with one of the principals like Jeremy Blanton or someone else with more experience, she would be less nervous. But then I noticed she was shaking in her solo work, too. She didn't last long as dancer.

I soon settled into company life, and that first year was a romp. I just loved being in the corps de ballet. It didn't matter at all whether I got to do solos, which was just as well, because my roles were all the standard corps de ballet parts: courtiers, peasants, and entertainers. I had always wanted to be a top dancer, but for now the back row was just fine. I felt the world was out there for me because I was in a ballet company. I didn't have to wear a tie and jacket and grey slacks and brown oxfords, and I didn't have to do school work or live in residence any more. I had my own bachelor apartment at Church and Isabella, a third-floor walk-up with a tiny window facing onto Church Street. I was immensely proud of it, although I couldn't really sleep well there because it was so noisy. I enjoyed a friendly competition with the other male dancers, who all seemed to take challenges in a fairly light-hearted way. I danced with some beautiful women. All this, and I got to travel, too.

My introduction to touring came that first winter, and it couldn't have been better. The American Southwest can look very attractive to Canadians in January, and to a young corps dancer who had never been out of the country or on a plane, the sight of palm trees and the sun in Tucson, Arizona, was little short of a miracle. I didn't mind the high-school gymnasiums and less-than-first-rate theatres we got to play — everything was new, and I lapped it all up. We weren't always brilliant on that tour. In fact, there were occasions when we were downright terrible, and one particularly sticks in my mind.

It was in Las Vegas, and just about everything went wrong. You could see people were forgetting entrances and steps, there were numerous technical mistakes, all bad enough that even I could see them. Celia was pretty angry, and from the men's dressing room after the performance, we could hear her screaming at the women across the hall, tearing a strip off them all. Then, hearing the clicking of her heels coming down the hallway, we all with one mind ran into the bathroom. She came into the dressing room, only to find it deserted. We were all in the toilets, three to a stall, standing on the seats, hiding. "Boys," she said to total silence. "Boys." She came through the dressing room into the bathroom area. "Boys," she said again to no response. We were frozen still, in precarious balance, desperately trying not to giggle or fall. Celia knew we were there, but she waited a moment, then turned and walked out. She had done what she needed to do to get her anger out with the girls. I'd like to think that, as she was walking away down the hallway, she was laughing at the idea of twenty young men feeling the need to hide from her. She could always be brought to laughter more easily with men than with women.

Celia gave me my first real solo the following summer, in Peter Wright's *Giselle*. It was during one of the company's performances at Ontario Place, in a small-but-showy role, the peasant pas de deux. I danced with Mary Jago, then a soloist and a much more experienced dancer, who was enormously generous and helpful to me. It was my first real opportunity to stand out, and I decided to go for broke. The performance wasn't perfect, but my enthusiasm and energy came through, and the audience responded. This chance to shine brought my first real taste of applause, and I found that I liked it. It changed my rather easygoing attitude. Enough of all these courtiers and peasants, I thought. I've spent enough time in the corps. Luckily for me, at the end of that first year, I was promoted to soloist at the tender age of eighteen.

That second year, I got to learn a little more about company life. For one thing, I found out just how frugal Celia could be. I was cast in a Roland Petit ballet, *Le Loup*, in which I played the wolf. "There's no money in the budget for fangs," Celia announced. So I set out on a mission to get my own. At the local joke shop, I bought a set – big ones. Fangs that could be seen from the back row of the O'Keefe Centre. With a carving tool, a thin drill bit, and fine wire, I formed my new fangs to fit perfectly over my own eye teeth. They worked magnificently, but only for as long as I maintained an enormous grin. Looking at myself in the mirror, I was horrified at what I saw. Staring back at me was a cross between a walrus and a sabre-toothed tiger. All I had to say was "Oh my God," and the beautiful fangs I had so lovingly altered came crashing to the floor.

Above: With Mary Jago in Le Loup. *The custom-made fangs had the benefit of staying in place.*

Below: An early solo at Ontario Place.

The next morning I marched into Celia's office, full of frustration and rage, and threw my very strange contraption, which by now looked like a bizarre tropical insect, on her desk. "Darling, what is that?" she asked. I calmed down a little and explained to Miss Franca that it had taken me two whole days to make my own fangs for *Le Loup* and that they didn't work. I could see she was trying not to laugh. I went on to say that I needed a professionally made set of fangs, like the ones I saw Jean-Pierre Bonnefous, one of Roland Petit's dancers, wear when he guested with the company. I told her I had found a Dr. Cramer who could construct them for $1,500. "We just don't have that kind of money in the budget," she claimed. "Couldn't you just paint them on?" But she knew that wasn't a good idea, and in the end gave me the go ahead to get my fangs custom-made. Aside from my ballet shoes and my fangs, all the costumes I wore were shared. I was very proud of my fangs; they brought a whole new dimension to the role.

Not that everyone appreciated them. Mary Jago and I danced the pas de deux at a local high school, and, although the dancing went well, the auditorium full of high-school students giggled and sneered like a pack of wolves themselves. The fangs were funny, but so was the pas de deux, which, unfortunately, didn't work well out of context. I felt dejected and humiliated, but Mary saw the funny side. She stood there in the wings, holding her sides, doubled over in an uncontrollable fit of laughter. I could see a bit of the humour in this, but it was another year before I could really see the funny side. Nobody at school had told me that this was what professional life would be like.

For the most part, I loved the dancer's life – the days that began not with coffee or tea, but with the daily ritual of class. I was always among the last to settle down to the introverted state that overtakes all dancers as they move through the early barre exercises. Slowly, my body would start to warm up, but it would not be until about fifteen minutes into class, when we got to fondus, which prepare you for jumping and landing, that I would really begin to feel I was getting in tune. By the time it came to move to the centre, I was ready for action. With centre exercises, everyone seemed to have marked out a piece of territory. I liked to work off-centre, slightly to stage right, and close to the front. I always hated working with someone in front of me, partly because to have no one there simulates a performance. I always looked forward to this part of class, when we got to do all the jumping, twisting, and turning steps. By the end of the hour or so of class, the day had begun. Class hones your body for the physical demands placed on it, but it is more than that. This is where, every day, you rededicate yourself to your art. It is extremely demanding but, young and healthy as I was, I felt wonderful when it was done. Class would be followed by rehearsals, which could occupy the whole day. Only on performance days did the round vary.

My second year in the company, I was given several new roles, including *The Mirror Walkers* and *Intermezzo*. Despite – or perhaps because of – my newfound ambition, the year wasn't great. I was getting more responsibilities, and being given roles that I really wasn't ready for. My technique also left a lot to be desired; there were things that, as a company member, I should have been able to do, and couldn't. Example: I wasn't able to accomplish a consistent double tour en l'air, which should be a fundamental for all male dancers. Fifty per cent of the time I'd land on my feet, the other fifty per cent I'd be shooting off in all directions. That was in the studio – in performance, it was even less consistent because, with all the adrenalin, you give 150 per cent, and you throw your body off even further. I was not the only company member with an inconsistent double tour, but somehow not being alone did not seem to help.

With steps still to master, adrenalin to control, and new, larger roles to learn, anxiety crept in. I started wondering if I was going to be good enough. Would I measure up for the audience and for Celia

With Mary Jago, in The Mirror Walkers.

Franca? I didn't want to embarrass myself and the company and I certainly didn't want to get heck from Celia. Then, along with my rekindled ambition and the worry it brought, I developed a tremendous sense of urgency. At the age of eighteen, I was suddenly a young man in a hurry. At that time, it was common for dancers to retire by the age of thirty-five. That wasn't complicated math — even I, with my abysmal 22 per cent, could do that. Seventeen years to make my mark. I had to start doing it fast. Anything that hadn't happened already had to happen tomorrow. Otherwise, I was convinced, it might never happen at all.

What was to become one of the most important relationships of both my personal and professional life began during that second season. Karen Kain has now become a national icon, the first home-based Canadian ballerina to develop a truly international following. Her talent and reputation as a dancer are without equal, and her name and face are recognized across the country. She has been acclaimed in almost everything she ever danced, showered with honorary degrees, partnered by some of the greatest dancers of her day. How then, with all this, can I try to recapture who she was then, when I first met her, before this all happened, when Karen was just Karen? Shy Karen, the Karen with all those doubts about whether she really could be good.

I had seen her in school, but I didn't know her. She was my senior, and in school, seniors didn't talk to juniors, and juniors didn't talk to seniors, that's just the way it was. Karen was just one of the bunheads, her hair pulled back, braces on her buck teeth, small alien ears and large facial features. At first I thought she had an odd, almost grotesque, look to her. Her memory of me is equally unflattering. To her, I was scrawny, with thick glasses, stringy hair, and chipmunk cheeks. Betty Oliphant had pointed me out to her when I was twelve, and she was fifteen. "I want you to see this new discovery," Betty had said to Karen, and then had repeated her favourite line, "he's going to be the new Erik Bruhn." Karen says that all she saw was this skinny thing with no technique.

Karen had arrived in the company a year ahead of me, and, until we were put together as regular partners in 1972, neither of us really expressed any interest in getting to know each other at all. I was more interested in her then-boyfriend, Timothy Spain, who I thought was great, with an interesting group of friends. Hanging around with these sophisticated guys appealed to me far more than hanging around with Karen.

Karen had been given a leading part in a new ballet, *The Mirror Walkers*, when she was still in the corps de ballet. Celia realized she needed a partner for Karen roughly Karen's age, with the same schooling and technical abilities, and it was soon clear she had me in mind. Like Karen, I also had a role in *The Mirror Walkers*, a minor one. Mary Jago and I were the reflections of Jeremy Blanton and Karen, and, thanks to Mary, I had shown myself to be at least an adequate partner. Mary had managed, if I was doing something that wasn't quite right, to gently suggest what I should do, which I imagine must have been frustrating for her at times, although she handled it with great tact. When it came time for me to work with Karen, I was no longer entirely green.

Our first serious work together was in Eliot Feld's *Intermezzo*. Feld, who been a dancer in the Broadway production of *West Side Story*, was just then getting established as a choreographer, a young, thirty-year-old New Yorker with a string of small works behind him. He had recently mounted this wonderful ballet, a series of waltzes set to the music of Brahms. Celia loved *Intermezzo* and invited Eliot to bring it to the National Ballet. He arrived to rehearse with us in the summer of 1971.

Eliot Feld is a brilliant and talented choreographer, but he turned out to be a mean individual. I don't know if he was like this with his own company, but with our company, he was a very hard task-master. He first chose six dancers for the work — Sergiu Stefanschi and Veronica Tennant, Jacques Gorrissen and Mary Jago, and Karen and me. As Eliot began teaching us the steps, he also began manipulating us psychologically. He constantly, on a daily basis, broke us down. He was very touchy, with a hair-trigger temper, and ultra-critical. Anything we did, even a beginning movement, he would stop and criticize. We endured some weeks of what amounted to emotional torture. Every day, one or more of the women would be crying because of what he said. His comments would be intensely personal, going to the core of who we were as dancers. I don't remember any of the men in tears, but some choice words were used to describe him in the locker room. But we'd grit our teeth and get back at it, because we wanted that choreography and couldn't wait to perform what was really a wonderful ballet. We all had respect for the ballet, and that's what kept us going back into the studio. After all these years, I can still say that he was worse than anything I've seen since.

Although his attacks were mostly on the women, Eliot also had problems with the men. He went for Sergiu Stefanschi, who was the most experienced, worked well, and had good waltzing and lifting technique. Eliot tried to get him out of what he saw as Sergiu's Soviet style, which he had learned in Romania and at the Kirov. Jacques Gorrissen – who has a temper to match Eliot's, the Taurus that he is – resisted at every moment. My approach was simply to keep my head down, get the steps, and do what he asked me to do. He realized that I was the youngest and most inexperienced dancer there, and his attacks on me were not as severe as on the others.

To tell the truth, Eliot could have been forgiven for losing it with me, because he had a big problem on his hands. These dances were waltzes, and I couldn't waltz. Try as I might, I just couldn't do it. I was particularly hopeless at waltzing with someone else, leading a partner, which is, of course, the point of the whole thing. The backwards and forwards motion would not come. I tried Eliot's patience here, and I also tried Karen's sorely. As a result, one of her first impressions of me was that I was painfully slow at learning steps. That wasn't always the case, but in this instance, she was right.

As it happened, I didn't get to dance on opening night in *Intermezzo*, since I had hurt my back. I was disappointed. The ballet went over really well with audiences and critics; it was compared to masterpieces like Jerome Robbins's *Dances at a Gathering*. That must have been pretty heady stuff for Eliot, and, in the end, he was pleased with us. Although he was, and still is, a wonderful choreographer, I was angry with him for the manner in which he treated us, and I felt I never wanted to work with him again. Many years later, I saw him at his studio in New York. Karen was guesting with him, and I had gone to the studio to visit. "Frank, you're man," he said, as I walked in, still his old abrasive self. "Eliot, you're old," was all I could think of to say back.

The next big opportunity to work with Karen came, as they so often do, when someone else was injured, and had to be replaced at the last minute. In April 1972, Karen was scheduled to dance her first performance of Juliet, in John Cranko's *Romeo and Juliet*, with Laszlo Surmeyan, one of the established principals in the company. About a week before the performance, Laszlo was injured, and Celia in her infinite wisdom decided that this was a role I could learn in a week. It was an extraordinary chance to perform one of the great works in the National's repertoire, although, with only one year of professional experience and a solitary week to rehearse, I may have been overly ambitious. We rehearsed endlessly, and I got to the point where I just about had the steps in my head. It helped that I loved the ballet, but I could hardly say that at the end of the week I was really ready to perform it.

Cranko had taken the pas de deux to another level with this ballet. For an inexperienced partner like me, this was definitely jumping in at the deep end. There is not that much solo dancing for the man in Cranko's version of the ballet, and what there is, is not as difficult as in, say, Kenneth MacMillan's version. However, because of the nature of the pas de deux in the first act, you need tremendous stamina. The lifts are extraordinarily difficult, and require

With Karen Kain, Romeo and Juliet.
Inset: As Romeo, in Romeo and Juliet.

that your timing be completely in tune with your partner's. If it is
off, the lifts take a lot more energy and can be downright dangerous.
This is some of the most difficult pas de deux work in the repertoire. Only an innocent or a fool would try to master it in a week.

As I was getting ready for that performance, there were days when
my back really ached. I was too young to have the sense to mark something first, so I went full out all the time. Karen and I both gave our
hearts and souls to our first performance, as if it was the last ballet we
would ever do. Earl Kraul had assured me that, after the first act is
over, acts two and three are easier. Your arms and legs are going to be
dead, but don't worry. He was right – even with the adrenalin rush, I
was exhausted. At the end of the first-act pas de deux, I barely had the
energy to lift Karen and put her back on the balcony, do the chin-up
kiss, pick up my cape, and run off. Earl caught me in the wings – if he
hadn't, I'd have collapsed to the floor. The second act was easier, and
the third, easier still. In both these acts, there was time to recover.
Laszlo Surmeyan, injured and watching from the sidelines, also tried
to help me in his enthusiastic way. "If this happens," he said, warning
me about a potential mishap, "don't be afraid." That was Laszlo.
Telling me everything to be afraid of. Until he mentioned it, it hadn't
occurred to me to be afraid of anything.

Karen and I both thought it went extremely well, and Celia and
our coaches were pleased. Still, there had been a few glaring mistakes.
For example, in the last pas de deux, at a point where we were to run
diagonally downstage, we ran into each other, my feet got caught
under hers, and she went tumbling down. It was one of those disas-
ters that there was absolutely no hiding – you just had to brush yourself off, get up, and continue. Generally, though, we felt good, because
we thought that we'd made an excellent beginning.

That feeling of accomplishment was short-lived. A few days later,
a review was due to come out. We were driving to the theatre, and, as
we were coming down Parliament Street in my Honda Civic, Karen

said "Let's get the *Globe and Mail.*" I drove, and Karen read our first review out loud. It was terrible. Critic Barbara Gail Rowes absolutely destroyed us. "Twenty-year-old Karen Kain and eighteen-year-old Frank Augustyn just weren't made for each other, at least not on ballet's stage," was her blunt verdict, writing the partnership off before it had even begun. Karen was too much woman for me, she said, and besides, she couldn't act. Karen by this time was crying; she couldn't finish the review. I stopped the car. We both felt we'd rather do anything but go back and do it again. If we were that bad, after working so hard, what more could we give? Clearly, it didn't work, why bother doing it at all?

We talked each other into taking the car the last 150 metres to the theatre, and there everyone was very supportive, making the usual noises about critics not knowing what they are talking about. Eventually we developed enough courage to go on and do another show – and that was a good thing. It helped us to understand that you should not grant one person the power to affect you in that way. Time and experience give you a thicker skin where critics are concerned, but at the beginning of a career, you are very vulnerable.

At the end of my second season with the company, we set out on our first European tour. I had never visited Europe before, and the trip was spoiled for me at the outset by a bout of flu. Instead of exploring, I could barely make it through class and rehearsal. The London reviews tell me that I was "an extremely promising young dancer who is fast and elegant." That's nice to know, but all I can recall of the tour is steadily getting warmer as we moved south, from London to Stuttgart to Lausanne, and at last, to the sun in Monte Carlo. Here we all got sunburns on the beach, and had to struggle into our tight *Intermezzo* jackets in excruciating pain. Celia was unsympathetic. She did not like sunburned dancers. We were, she quite rightly thought, unaesthetic.

CHAPTER

4

The Mentor

In the early 1970s, there were two other large ballet companies in Canada, the Royal Winnipeg Ballet and the Grand Ballets Canadien of Montreal. At that time, each had a big box-office drawing card: the Royal Winnipeg was performing *Ecstasy of Rita Joe*, a dramatic work telling the story of a native girl coming to the city, and the Grand Ballets had *Tommy*, to music by The Who. Both were extremely popular with the public, and Celia was looking around for an equivalent draw for the National. This led to a deal in which all our fates were to be radically changed. Sol Hurok, the New York impresario, agreed to take on the National Ballet of Canada, as a backdrop to his real star, Rudolf Nureyev. Hurok was then the leading ballet promoter in the world, and his support with the presence of Nureyev meant an entree into major opera houses worldwide. Under the terms of the deal, Rudolf Nureyev

Rudolf Nureyev, trademark tuque in place, taking a rehearsal.

59

would come to Canada to mount a new production of *Sleeping Beauty*, and the company would tour this production, with Nureyev in the leading role. The tour would culminate with the company's first season at the Metropolitan Opera House in New York.

We first got to hear about this turn of events in Vancouver, at the Queen Elizabeth Theatre in February 1971. Celia took Karen and me off to the side of the stage. She looked very tired and drawn, and she was clearly very upset. "I love you both," she said. "The company looks so wonderful and the two of you look so wonderful together. I think I've made a terrible mistake." Karen and I were still only twenty and eighteen, and our sole experience of Celia had been as the Dragon Lady. What awful mistake was she about to confess, as she stood holding back tears in front of us? "I've just sold the company," she said.

"What do you mean?" I managed to ask.

"I've just signed a contract with Sol Hurok and Nureyev. It means $40,000 a week for the next year, and the company will survive." That was a bit of a shock. It had never occurred to me that the company might not survive, but it was then on shaky financial ground. Celia was in the bad books of her board, who wanted to get her out. Those words still resonate: "I've sold the company." What she meant was she had given up control of the company to Sol Hurok. He would pay all the bills, and everyone would always get paid. There was a price: instead of the National Ballet of Canada, for the next few years, it would seem more like Rudolf Nureyev and company. Critic William Littler said that, for Sol Hurok, the National Ballet of Canada was the parsley surrounding the fish. He was not far wrong.

In summer of 1972, Rudolf Nureyev arrived at our studios to work on the new production. He was then at the height of his career, still dancing at the top of his form, while also mounting new productions for companies around the world. He had gone his own freelance route, never tying himself down to one company, and his blazing talent, combined with his compulsive work habits, had made him the biggest star the art form had ever had. Certainly he was the only male dancer whose name was a household word. Seven years earlier I had bought his picture at Hamilton Centre Mall and hung it on my bedroom wall. Now, I was about to dance with him. Like all male dancers I was in awe of him, not only because he was a wonderful dancer, but also because he made a lot of money doing it. This wasn't something many dancers managed to do – certainly not at the National Ballet of Canada. Most of us were downright poor.

That first day, the energy level in the studio was very high. He arrived looking very svelte, in tight-fitting clothing, a pair of old, well-worn boots, and, as always, his trademark tuque. Everyone was keen to dance the best they could for this legend, whose aura seemed to expand the entire studio. Casting for *The Sleeping Beauty*, with Celia Franca by his side, he pointed his finger at Karen and at me. "Put on page," he said in his heavy Russian accent, while Celia's assistant busily made notes. Rudolf hadn't seen the two of us dance together; he chose us individually. He said my name with a twang and a grimace, as if he found it ugly. He wasn't particularly interested when Celia went on to point out some of the company's established stars – his interest was more in discovery. Karen and I were interesting to him because we were young and unknown. I think Rudolf liked to claim he had discovered us, but really and truly, it was Celia Franca and Betty Oliphant who did this. I left the session knowing I was being cast for something, although I didn't know what. The next day I came to rehearsal to find out that I would be doing a pas de cinq, a Rose Adagio courtier, and Bluebird. It was Bluebird I was interested in, a small role with a big reputation, demanding both in style and stamina. I was pleased to be cast in it because I knew that it would show off one of my best qualities, my elevation. In the beginning, I didn't get to dance with Karen, but happily with Mary Jago, whose good speed and precision made her a beautiful Princess Florine.

*In this studio picture you can almost feel
the excitement Rudolf's presence made.
Veronica Tennant is in the foreground;
Karen Kain and Vanessa Harwood are to her left.*

I had learned sections of Bluebird, and thought I knew the piece. However, when Rudolf arrived to rehearse us, I was in for a shock. The men all went upstage left, where we usually started the variation, to begin the diagonal. We were huddled in the corner, at the ready, when Rudolf pointed to the other corner. That threw everyone off balance — we had to start at the corner we weren't used to starting at, the one we found harder. Then we discovered why. He had kept two diagonals in the variation, the way Tchaikovsky originally wrote it. Rudolf wanted to make the production as long as possible, and if Tchaikovsky wrote it that way, then that's the way it would be: right and left, and very demanding. It is hard to do this variation and do it well, and all too easy to make it look ridiculous. The pas de poisson, the first step, can look downright silly when not done with the necessary lightness. When it works, Bluebird is a magical piece for the audience, but for the dancer it is an aerobic killer. It is also very, very hard to get the style right. In some ways it is harder than dancing the Prince, because it is far more stylized, and for the nine minutes you are on, you go full out all the time. When you do that, nine minutes does not seem such a short time.

Three couples were cast in the role. The big issue was who would get to do it on opening night, and Rudolf chose me and Mary Jago. I found it was an interesting part to interpret — the whole look that a man could give to a birdlike creature without looking like a fugitive from *Swan Lake*. I found different ways I could play with my arms and head, and the steps seemed to come very naturally to me. I loved the jumping, and being able to use the torso. Bluebird can steal the show, if the leads, the Prince and Aurora, are not strong. It was a great opportunity. Rudolf taught from his vision of the Kirov version, which was part memory and part his own imagination. He was specific and detailed about everything: arms, head, feet, and legs — all had to be just right, and worked together intricately. I didn't know at the time that his version was unique. It was only after seeing many other stagings of it that I realized how special Rudolf's staging was. All I knew was that I was nineteen and working with Rudolf Nureyev, the biggest star in ballet. Life could not have been better.

Rudolf was to have a major influence on my development as a dancer. There was so much I admired about him. To me he seemed the ultimate symbol of masculine strength and virility in dance. He had beauty, talent, and drive, and a total dedicated passion for dance. He also had a fierce desire to be noted, to be recognized. As I got to know him over the next few years, I was never one hundred per cent sure that Rudolf's passion for dance was greater than his passion for being noticed. Before his arrival on the ballet scene, the male dancer was typically regarded as a secondary character. Rudolf changed two things here: first, his personal style was an eye-opener in the West, it was so explosive and strong. Rudolf brought the male dancer out of the background and into the limelight. He was a good partner, true, but there was more, far more, to his dancing abilities than being a *porteur*. He gave all male dancers something new to aim for – the standards were raised, both for partnering and solo work. Secondly, in order to give expression to his ability, he made changes in the classical repertoire to give more dancing to the man. This was a new era for male dancers. I was enormously lucky to have arrived when I did, and even luckier to now be working directly with the man who had started the whole process.

It was a time in my life when I needed someone to look up to. Rudolf and his whole manner of movement seemed to me to be so right that I did the obvious thing. I copied him. I'm a good mimic, and for a period of about two and a half years, I mimicked him, in every detail. In some of the photographs I see of myself from that time, I even start to look like him. That was the result of a conscious effort. Everything about him fascinated me – the way he carried himself, the way he worked, the way he looked. He had such an interesting and compelling face, such a charming – if temperamental – personality. I tried to work the way he worked, physically and mentally. I tried to understand the way his mind worked, to get under his skin, and I set out to place his manner of movement onto my own body. The only thing I didn't copy was his approach to jumping, which I didn't like, as his landings were very heavy. Betty Oliphant saw what I was doing and warned me to take the good things from him, but not the bad things, which for her meant the jumping and some aspects of his behaviour which we later got to know about. For those two and half years I was under his spell. Only then did I gradually begin to move away from imitation to allow my own style and natural qualities to come through.

Rudolf had been sufficiently unsure of the quality of male dancing in the company that he had hired Georges Piletta of the Paris Opéra Ballet as a guest artist for that first season, knowing that, with him, he could at least be sure of one good Bluebird. At the time, Piletta was paid more than any of the other dancers, yet in a four-and-a-half month, thirty-two-city tour, he did maybe three performances. Rudolf got tired of him, and, as a result, I did the bulk of the Bluebirds. That was fine with me, not so fine for Georges. To his enduring credit, Piletta worked with us with incredible dignity. He accepted the fact that roles were moving away from him, but he had a contract, and he was committed to stay, so stay he did. With extraordinary grace, he did not ever turn his back on me, even though he had cause to do so.

A lot has been written about the risk the National Ballet took with *The Sleeping Beauty*. It was an extraordinarily opulent, expensive production, and to this day audiences still gasp when the curtain goes up to reveal the costumes and sets. Watching the production come together was something of an eye-opener for dancers who had, until then, counted frugality as a company watchword. It was a dramatic turnabout from the joke-shop fangs of only a year before.

Rudolf chose Nicholas Georgiadis to design the sets and costumes. They had worked together before, on a production of *Swan Lake* for the Vienna Opera, and *Raymonda* and *The Sleeping Beauty* for the Zurich Ballet. Georgiadis was a great spender, thinking nothing of using real feathers and leather and silks and brocades. He would go out shopping with the

Nicolas Georgiadis's spectacular costumes for The Sleeping Beauty.

head of wardrobe, James Ronaldson, and Ronaldson, used to a more modest, Canadian approach to materials, would suggest imitation silk and leather. But no, it had to be the best, and if you didn't get it right the first time, then throw it out, and start again. When Rudolf first looked at the assembled set for the birthday scene, in which an enormous curved staircase sweeps down across the stage, he turned to Georgiadis. "Where is the stage for me to dance, Georgio?" he asked. He was right — architecturally, it looked great, but there was no stage left to dance on. Three pillars were thrown out and the whole thing redone to make room for us to perform. Georgiadis spent with abandon — which is easy to do, after all, when the money isn't yours.

Costume changes were common. When Rudolf saw the costumes for Carabosse's monster attendants in the first act, he yelled at Georgiadis, "These don't look like monsters at all!" The costumes were too new and not scary enough. It was too late to make new ones, so Georgiadis took a torch to them and singed them. This was real velvet and brocade, singed, to make it look old. To dancers used to wearing the simple and generally very inexpensive — though well-made — costumes from the company's wardrobe department, this was extravagant, if not downright wasteful. Then again, since we were to open in Ottawa, the whole production was built for the National Arts Centre, which was unique in Canada in terms of its large size, and the kind of sets it could accommodate. Nothing was designed for touring, so even more money had to be spent in recreating everything so that we could tour.

Throughout the rehearsal period, Celia and Rudolf gave each other a wide berth. I think Rudolf respected Celia, but didn't like it if she tried to meddle in his choreography and decisions. He wanted her to direct the company and leave him alone. She found him a necessary evil, as, I think, he did her. He used to call her Pizzdelia. At the time, none of us really knew what he meant, but we later found out that *pizzda* in Russian means a certain part of the female anatomy, or whore. He did that to a lot of people; he would use Russian swear words interlocked

As the Prince, in The Sleeping Beauty. *I wore the wig only once.*

with a person's name. Celia in turn respected him, but I'm not sure that she liked him, if for no other reason than the control he demanded. This was her company, she had founded it, nurtured it, brought it to maturity. Now, she felt as if this upstart superstar was calling all the shots. To add to the irritation, she had to find the money to pay for all the grand ideas, and the expense was mounting daily. So much money was being spent, but the point of no return was long gone. Celia and the board were in far too deep to get out. The chairman of the board, Paul Deacon, and his wife, Adele, mortgaged their house to finance the production, which, if nothing else, showed an extraordinary level of faith in the whole effort.

The first performance was in Ottawa, in September 1972. I danced the Bluebird with Mary Jago. Later, I started to perform it more and more with Karen. When we danced it together, a lot of people found it impressive, so, slowly but surely, Rudolf saw to it that Karen and I were seen together more in the roles.

The Sleeping Beauty was the centrepiece of the repertoire we took on a four-month North American tour with Nureyev, which culminated at the Metropolitan in New York. It was a gruelling tour, the hardest the company had ever undertaken. Rudolf was dancing every night, eight shows a week, and so was I. I spent most of that tour on Aspirin. I was young, but you can't perform eight shows a week and not be hurting. All the company was dancing all the time – when the ballerinas were not dancing Aurora, they would take the role of one of the fairies. Soloists when not doing solos would take on corps roles. And the corps, of course, were always on.

According to his contract, Sol Hurok had to have Nureyev on stage every night, but there were a few nights when he just couldn't do it. Those were the nights I got. So I did the Prince in *Sleeping Beauty*, or the Prince in *Swan Lake*, or Don Juan, or Albrecht in *Giselle*. The hardest days for me were when I did the Prince at the matinee, and then returned to do Bluebird in the evening. Although Rudolf had fewer nights off than I, he had a very solid, durable body. It was harder on me, partly because my body was not as durable and partly because I didn't have the experience to pace myself. With me, it was all or nothing. I did every show as though it were a matter of life and death. My nerves too, were a problem. I was so anxious to go out and do well. It didn't matter to me if it were Iowa or New York, I gave the same one hundred per cent. Then I watched Rudolf, and I learned quite a bit, because that was not how he approached it.

When we did Toronto, and Vancouver, and San Francisco, he was great. Then we started into the Midwest, and I saw his performance level drop. He played with it. He arrived at the theatre as the performance began, did his warm-up while the performance was going on, then he'd get on stage, do the first few solos more or less as warm-up. It was very reserved; he'd be holding himself back. Always he was the performer, but physically he wasn't doing everything full out. But never, ever, in the third act. With that variation in the grand pas de deux, he'd pull out all the stops. Always, with that solo he would bring the house down, every time, guaranteed – and he knew it. In Chicago, three weeks before New York, he started building himself up again, and each performance got better and better. When we got to New York, he was at his very best.

As for everyone else, the show was always good, because if it wasn't you'd hear about it from him. His eyes were everywhere. I think it was in Cleveland, after what felt like the two hundredth performance of the Bluebird, that he let me know just how much he was watching us. Just before the finale, at the top of the grand staircase before we all made our final curtain-call entrance, he looked at me.

"Are you bored?" he asked.

"No, I'm not bored," I said. "I'm tired."

He just held my gaze, as if to say, What's tired? As if no one could know fatigue like he knew fatigue. "You? Tired?" he said. "Well, get used to it." I felt it was a put-down. And I *was* tired. Maybe my performance level was not what it should have been. I presumed from that comment that he wasn't happy with me. But, after the final performance of Bluebird in Toronto, he said that I was the best Bluebird in the world. "Not quite like Soloviev," he added, "but today, you are the best Bluebird in the world." That was praise I valued, because Rudolf did not throw compliments around lightly. He was the most honest man I ever met, and if he said something, I knew he meant it.

Early on in the tour, I was taken out of other smaller roles to concentrate more on the Prince. This was so new. I had never done anything like it before, and I didn't know how to handle myself. This was only my second year in the company, and I was being given principal roles at what was a very young age. It was an uncertain time, because I never knew when I would be called on to actually dance. It wasn't uncommon to be woken up at nine o'clock in the morning and told, You're on, do the matinee. It could be with any one of the five company ballerinas, and they all had their own way, their style, their own levels of jumping, weight, height, and size. This was a problem for me, because I still hadn't done a lot of partnering. There was one day when I partnered Veronica Tennant, who is five foot three, followed by Karen, who is five foot seven. I partnered Veronica in the matinee. At one point I lifted her, and thought I had put her down, only to realize she wasn't on the ground as she came down with a thump. I had misjudged the height. I'd just got used to Veronica, and then in the evening I partnered Karen, and the first lift I did I smashed her into the ground. That was the only time that happened. The lesson learned in partnering: know your ballerina's height.

I was lucky to escape Nureyev's eagle eye on this one, for he could be brutal when others made mistakes. On one occasion, in the second act of *The Sleeping Beauty*, the lights came on too soon, and the audience saw Nureyev climbing stairs which he should have been seen descending. He was furious and started yelling and screaming – more than enough to wake up the dancers, who in the story are supposed to be waking from a hundred-year sleep. He went up to two dancers and banged their heads together like coconuts. There he was, walking around the stage yelling, "Fucking shit, lights too bright, why?" This in a performance, in front of an audience. Vanessa Harwood was the princess, and instead of giving her a kiss to wake her up, he first lifted her torso off the bed, then kissed her dramatically and held the kiss for a very long time, with the music going. As a result, everything was late. Everyone had to run to make the final pose.

Later in Chicago, something else was wrong. I heard Rudolf screaming at Ernie Abugov, the stage manager, about the lights. I looked out of my dressing room, and saw him go to a corkboard on the wall, and start banging his head against it. "Get Frank," he yelled, "I not do fucking performance." I quickly ducked back into my dressing room. I didn't want to be in range, and I certainly didn't want to have to go on at such short notice.

These explosions would often happen before performances. He would get upset about something, I think partly to get himself going. He was bored and tired, and he needed the adrenalin. No one, not even Rudolf Nureyev, should do eight performances a week, certainly not with the performance expectations placed on him. Of course, no one made him do this number of performances. He wanted and needed to perform, but it was still stressful. He knew he was getting paid handsomely, and that he had better produce. Anger was just a way of releasing all the pressure. He would always be late getting on stage. He'd start getting dressed only bars before he had to go on, and then get mad at his dresser because his dresser wasn't moving fast enough. He was deliberately putting himself into a position of jeopardy. Of course, no one else had the right to behave that way. We all were terrified of not pleasing him — we were so young, and naïve, and impressionable.

Opening night in New York went well, with even the usually hard-to-please *New York Times* critic, Clive Barnes, giving the company a good review. I was happy to be called a dancer of "outstanding promise," and a little less happy to be told I'd be better when I learned to point my feet! Karen and I were given one matinee to do in the lead roles, which was advertised and pushed very heavily. Sol Hurok was canny enough to realize that something was going on when we danced together. We sold out the house, which thrilled everyone, because it said we didn't need Rudolf Nureyev to sell out the Met! Somehow, Karen and I got through it. With guts, I have to say. Karen did so with greater ease. She had danced this role with Rudi throughout the tour.

It was at the Met that summer that I finally learned how to apply stage make-up. We were never really taught how to do this, which was more of a problem for the men than the women, who seemed to absorb the skill by osmosis as a natural part of growing up. I was a hopeless case. Various members of the company tried to help me, but all that did was make me look like them. Laszlo Surmeyan decided to give me a hand, since he thought I was doing such a lousy job of it. He carefully gave me his shadowing, which worked beautifully for him with his dramatic nose, big jaw and heavy eyebrows. On me, it looked like clown make-up. I didn't want to hurt his feelings, so, when he left the dressing room, I made a few small adjustments. I still looked like a clown. From this I knew I couldn't learn from another dancer. Luckily, at the Met, the make-up artist took me into his room and applied my make-up for me. He explained what he was doing and why. That night, everyone complimented me on my performance. I swear it was because of the make-up. I no longer looked like a monster.

Our *Sleeping Beauty* tour was important for the National, and for the careers of many dancers. Although the production cost an enormous amount of money, at around $400,000 plus — almost twice its original budget — it was a very smart move for everyone. The company got into opera houses that had previously been out of reach, and its general status was raised several notches. The ballerinas all got great exposure and performing experience. Of the male dancers, I was perhaps the only one who really benefitted. I think I was Nureyev's first protégé, and I believe he wanted as much as possible to help. I really got the feeling that he cared about my development as an artist. In that way, I think there was generosity, but I also think he felt a certain pride, since I got better because of what he taught me. I was a symbol of his work, a talented young dancer he could mould.

The other male dancers felt a little as if they were being pushed aside. There were a lot of men in the company who knew they had more to offer than dancing as one of the courtiers in the Rose Adagio. One or two spoke up, suggesting they could be doing more. I was lucky to be cast more than I had any right to expect, given that it was only my second year in the company. I was also lucky that the other male dancers took this well. I never felt any sense of animosity or jealousy from them, even though I had been catapulted over them into the role of main back-up for Nureyev. Perhaps there was some-times a joking dig, but it didn't go very deep. Only one dancer seemed really to be bothered, and he turned to me after the casting list had been posted one day and said, "Who did you have to sleep with to get that?" I didn't even bother to answer. It was true, Nureyev pursued me – he was gay and I wasn't, and I think that intrigued him, and made it a bit of a challenge. But we came to an understanding. I am sure there were people within the company who really believed I was sleeping with him, and that was why I was cast in Bluebird and the Prince, and cast for opening night, but the people who really knew me realized it wasn't true. There were occasions when it bothered me, but mostly I didn't give it too much thought.

Nureyev was a natural flirt, with a voracious sexual appetite, and I think he probably tried with everyone. His blatant sexuality could embarrass people around him. He'd think nothing of pawing someone in a public place. He knew he could get away with it, and he liked living on an edge where he never knew what the answer would be or how far could he push. Fortunately, by the time he arrived on the scene, I had no doubts about my sexuality. The days of being worried about advances from the opera chorus were long over. I admired Nureyev, and thought he was very handsome, but I felt no sexual attraction to him. When he did make advances, they were always in play, in fun, and I would try to be playful back, saying, Not in this lifetime, buddy. We'd laugh and tease, and that's the way it was left. Generally, the advances were not subtle, and his language could at times be notoriously coarse. None of this disrupted the work in process. For Nureyev, work was work. We remained friends. I don't know that we could have spent two weeks on an island together and have had things to talk about, but there was a mutual respect and trust. If something went wrong, he'd be there to help, and if something went wrong with him, I'd be there, if I could be of help. That's how it unfolded.

When Rudolf Nureyev danced it was always a dance of pride, giving a feeling of something complete and whole about a man dancing. That was what I wanted. I saw right there before my eyes, in everything he did, what I was striving for. In all this, Rudolf exuded confidence, and confidence wasn't something that came naturally to me. I needed validation, and Rudolf's approval was the highest validation I could get. Rudolf Nureyev gave me something priceless at the very beginning of my career. He helped me believe in myself. On a purely technical level, he had an enormous influence on us all, making us all better than we were, but it went way beyond that. A truly gifted person and a natural leader, he had some special light inside that pervaded his entire being. I have met very few people in my life who were truly inspirational. Rudolf was one. I feel privileged to have known and worked with the man.

———————

5

The Competition

During the course of the *Sleeping Beauty* tour, Celia Franca asked Karen and me if we would like to compete in the Second Moscow International Ballet Competition. This was a relatively new event on the dance calendar – held only once before, in 1969, when Mikhail Baryshnikov won gold in the men's competition. Modelled on the competition of longer standing in Varna, Bulgaria, it was designed to give exposure to young dancers. Celia had been asked to be one of the sixteen judges, and she thought it would be good experience for Karen and me. I was too young for the senior category, although Karen, at twenty-two, was old enough. I should have entered as junior, but I couldn't if I were to partner her. So I entered as a senior instead, with a meagre one-and-a-half years' professional dancing experience. I was uncertain about going, and not at all sure that I was ready for it.

———————

Florestan from the Bluebird pas de deux. This image captures a sense of flight.

We began trying to rehearse during the tour with Nureyev, which proved very difficult, because we weren't always dancing the roles we were to compete with. Karen by that time had one season more than I as a professional dancer, plus she had worked in a greater variety of roles. I did a lot of Bluebirds, and some other minor roles, plus every once in a while I got to do the male lead in *Swan Lake*, and *The Sleeping Beauty*. That was about it.

After the season was over, we had two weeks to prepare. As the Russian stages were raked, the National Ballet's production crew tried to build a raked stage for us in the studio; it was tiny, and all we could really do was to stand on it and feel the angle. You have to throw your weight back when the stage is raked, because you are standing down-hill, which throws off your equilibrium. The worst for me was a manège, a jumping circle. You'd start downstage left, and going across at the bottom was not bad. But then, going upstage, it was a battle. Going across the top, your landing has to be adjusted, because you are landing downhill. Then you turn for the real downhill run, and you have to put the brakes on. It was very hard to get used to, and we were at a disadvantage, because the Russians in the competition lived with this on a daily basis.

Once we arrived we had other disadvantages. We were in a strange country, it was difficult to get any food, we were losing weight like mad, and, more importantly, because of the weight loss, we were losing energy. Then again, we weren't given the choice times to rehearse on stage: one rehearsal at three o'clock in the morning on the day of the first performance was all the stage time we got. The Russians and all the Soviet satellite countries were given prime times in both the theatre and the studio. We, on the other hand, had difficulty getting any studio time at all. In addition, the Russians were also dancing the pas de deux they were to perform year round. They had been in training for the competition for a whole year. Our only advantage — and it turned out to be a considerable one — was the meticulous training we had been given by Rudolf.

We had travelled to Moscow with the National's accompanist, Mary McDonald, and three dancers who had come to see the competition and take classes, Linda Maybarduk, Nadia Potts, and Wendy Reiser. Celia was unable to coach us, as she was judging, so a friend of hers, teacher and coach Eugen Valukin, came to look at us, and promptly started to change our choreography, which was the last thing we needed. We planned to do Bluebird, the *Sleeping Beauty* grand pas de deux, the Black Swan, and Roland Petit's *Le Loup*, fangs and all.

We stayed in Moscow for a total of three weeks, at the Rossiya Hotel, a drab glass, steel, and marble building near the Kremlin. Then only six years old, and boasting some six thousand rooms, it claimed to be the largest hotel in the world. That it may well have been, but it was certainly short on food. I was starving for almost the entire stay there; I lost a total of ten pounds, which on a lean frame of 153 pounds was a lot. It turned out that the best place to find food was in the canteen at the Bolshoi Theatre, but we weren't always at the theatre. Elsewhere, you could get an egg, bread, cucumbers, yogurt, and cheese and tea, and that was about it. At the theatre, performers could get meat, bacon, and many other things to eat, which we could buy at a subsidized price. We didn't get vegetables or greens, even though it was summer. I'd never seen anything like it, and no one had prepared us for it. We might have brought some food with us, if we had known. We had brought some Tang, for the vitamin C, and that was about it.

With little food in the hotel, Karen and I, naïve travellers that we were, thought we would try the restaurants, which were mostly empty. This should have been a signal that something was wrong. There would be this huge menu, and Karen, who knew a little Russian, would try to order. The waiter would come, and she'd say what we wanted, and it was always *nyet*. She'd choose again, and again the answer was *nyet, nyet*. Everything on the menu was *nyet*. Finally we'd say, bring us what you do have. One day what arrived was bread, cheese, and sturgeon, and we felt triumphant. Another time, we were not so lucky. We went into a restaurant, and they said they had chicken soup. So we got our soup, put in a spoon, and out came a wing, with feathers on it. They hadn't plucked the feathers off the chicken, which was enough to make you lose your appetite. We laughed a lot about it afterward. We had to, there was nothing else to do.

Throughout the preparation time, we more or less kept to ourselves. Occasionally, Alexander Godunov from the Bolshoi would come and practise his English on us, and we'd sometimes have lunch with Danish dancer Peter Schaufuss, who later became a principal with the National Ballet. Peter knew his way around a bit, as this was his second time in Moscow, and he was able to find a few restaurants that actually had food. Mostly, though, we were on our own.

Karen and I liked each other a lot, we were good friends, and I now found her very attractive. Part of the attraction was her liveliness and fearlessness – she was absolutely fearless in expressing what she felt on stage. I knew instinctively that she could help me out of my shell. Celia hastened matters along inadvertently one day. Worried that we were losing weight, and feeling that we might not have the stamina to make it through the competition, she had taken us back to her hotel to give us a meal. She was a judge, and she had a card that gave her more privileges than mere dancers, with access to more food. After a meal of soup and beef, she locked us in the same room together, saying, "And now you must rest." We took advantage of the opportunity – but not exactly the way she intended. That was the beginning of an affair that lasted, through many ups and downs, for seven years.

Between not having food, and not sleeping very well, and the weird hours of rehearsal times, we lived in a world of unbelievable tension.

Everything I looked at meant competition. My hotel room, the theatre, the studio, my partner: everything was a constant eighteen-hour-a-day reminder of competition. Nerves started getting to me. I dropped even more weight. Everything about Moscow seemed different. On our way to the theatre, I would walk directly in front of Karen, because men would deliberately bump into her. We stood out so in our blue jeans. We had an entirely different look, not only in what we wore, but also our expressions. You could see just by looking at their faces that the Russians were not happy.

For us, it was thrilling to see Red Square and St. Basil's, the beauty of it, awash in colour in the summer sun. The most depressing part of it all was coming back to the Rossiya Hotel, with the *dezhurnaya* taking your key and keeping a watch on all your comings and goings. We did a morning class at the Bolshoi, taught by Asaf Messerer, which I really enjoyed. Vladimir Vasiliev, Alexander Gordeyev, Maris Liepa, and Alexander Godunov were all in the company then – an extraordinary crop of talented male dancers. Messerer didn't say very much, but his combinations were incredible, and the general atmosphere of class was so good.

At the beginning of the competition, Karen and I were couple number twenty-six. The first round saw almost half of the seventy-three dancers in competition eliminated. We did the best number that we had, which was Bluebird, and successfully got through. What we didn't know at the time was that this first round was not marked for points. Had we known that, we would have saved this, our best, until the end, and done the *Sleeping Beauty* grand pas de deux. Because of this, we ended up doing the things we were less experienced in for the points. After the second round, there were more eliminations, and again, we made it through.

There were seven couples left in the final. Everyone chose the Black Swan pas de deux, keeping this most bravura of pas de deux to

With Karen Kain, the Bluebird pas de deux.

the end. The first couple came out, and did *Swan Lake*. Then the second couple came out, and the Black Swan music started again. By the time the third couple were on, the audience was groaning. With the fourth couple, the groans turned to laughter. Being couple number six didn't exactly help us. The only minor advantage we had was that we were using different music, which at least gave the audience musical relief. At the end of the day, I didn't think I had done that well. Karen didn't think she had, either. We saw some incredible dancers: Godunov, Gordeyeev, Nadezhda Pavlova, Semenyaka, Schaufuss – all these dancers were in their mid-twenties, approaching their prime. I think the oldest was twenty-eight. Peter Schaufuss was five years older than me, had entered the first Moscow competition, and was now back to compete again. This time, he was going for the gold, and was very disappointed to get silver, though realistically his chances for gold against Soviet dancers on home territory were incredibly slim. That was brought home to me when Gordeyeev and Godunov told me in the dressing room one day that they were going to win. Innocent Canadian that I was, I wondered how they could know. How could they be so sure?

Being among incredible dancers doing brilliant things, Karen and I wondered what we were doing there. As it turned out, Karen did very well, winning the silver medal, and I did well, too, placing only a fraction of a mark out of a bronze. But I didn't see that then, and neither did she. We felt we had let everyone around us down, that it was a disgrace not to get gold. I was given – I thought out of sympathy – the prize for the best couple, which was really more a special mention, as there really wasn't such a prize. We had all entered as individuals and were judged and marked individually. There were no medals given for pas de deux work. I was left with an overwhelming sense of defeat. It was a very discouraging time. I thought, How many shots like this do I get? My partner won something, and I didn't. When you look at it realistically and sensibly, it was damned good what I did as a junior in a senior competition. I should have been proud of myself. But I wasn't looking at anything realistically then. Celia Franca had warned us, before the competition started, that we would not win. We were just in for the experience. So, on one level, I was prepared not to win, but deep down inside, even if I knew this, I still wanted to. I carried a sense of failure with me for many years. My only small consolation was that, at the award ceremony, I was given a special mention and the audience applauded long and loud enough that I had to stand up and take two bows.

How you respond to competition depends, I think, very much on your temperament. It takes not only preparation but also a certain kind of attitude. Some dancers thrive on competition. Not me. I didn't go into ballet to compete. I went into to it to interpret something with my body and communicate with an audience. The only time I had done anything like this before was when I was a child. Then, if I remembered the steps, it was okay, and if I didn't, I improvised – and still won something. This was different. I thought nothing could be more nerve-racking than performing at the Met. I was wrong. Performing in competition was the most nerve-racking experience I could have gone through. The best thing about the entire experience was learning that I never wanted to do it again. Ever.

We left Moscow at the end of July, and when we landed in Paris, the first thing we did was order salad. We couldn't get enough fresh greens, which we hadn't seen in three long weeks. Now, we were free. I had not had time off in almost two years. We had gone straight from the European tour into rehearsals for *The Sleeping Beauty*. Then had come the regular season, followed by the long American tour, finishing off with the stress of Moscow. The summer break came as a welcome relief. It was one of the most memorable summers of my life, spent with friends and fellow dancers Linda Maybarduk and Frank Anderson, in Cagnes-sur-Mer, near Cannes, while Karen went to Paris to meet up with her then boyfriend. Our days passed in a haze of sun and sea and food, but there was always class, too. We were still young enough, and our bodies strong enough, to want to work every day without any rest. Even on vacation. The day would begin at the studio run by the American ballerina Rosella Hightower, which was known to dancers throughout Europe as a good place to take class. Then, it was off to the beach. Dancers from all over the world gathered here, the professionals with their own plot in the sand, the students and wannabe professionals further along the beach in another plot. Frank Anderson had rented a house from Peter Schaufuss, a small four-room dwelling with a door right on the road, high in the hills above Cannes. Linda and I left our dive of a hotel and moved in with him to save money, and for two weeks the three of us hung out together, travelling the countryside in Frank's tiny yellow Deux Chevaux, which could barely make it up the hill. A young American girl attached herself to our group, and when we moved on to Paris, this led to a scene that I will never forget. It was the only time in my life I have been involved in a pure French farce.

I had gone ahead to get tickets for an outdoor performance of *Swan Lake* that Rudolf was doing with Natalia Makarova at the Louvre. Linda and I were to meet up at our hotel (another dive), where to save money we were sharing a room, and had registered as Mr. and Mrs. Augustyn. Hard to believe it, but that was what you had to do then, even in Paris. Linda and I were not lovers, just good friends, but the concierge didn't know that.

I got tickets from Rudolf, and had only been back in my hotel room a few minutes when the American girl from Cannes showed up. I didn't know it, but she was following me. Slowly, it began to dawn on me that there was something going on here. We went sightseeing for a bit, and when it turned out that she didn't have money for a hotel, I reluctantly offered to share the room with her. Now I was definitely uncomfortable, making sure she slept in the bed, while I slept as far across the room from her as I could get, on a chair. The next morning, the concierge, who had seen us together, called in a panic to let me know that my wife (Linda) had arrived. I went bounding down the stairs, and hugged and kissed Linda – overjoyed that she was here to rescue me from this awful situation. All this was observed, in a spirit of some puzzlement, by the concierge. While this was going on, the American girl came down the stairs, and, to the amazement of the old lady, there were friendly hellos all round. Clearly, from the expression on her face, the concierge thought she had a very modern ménage booked into room twenty-one. She must have been even more amazed when we booked another room, which Linda shared not with me, but with the American girl. Linda and I later met up with Karen to see Rudolf's *Swan Lake*, performed in the open air before six thousand people in almost arctic temperatures.

On the plane back to Toronto, Karen and I received an unexpected invitation. Karen had fallen asleep, while I, with my usual trouble sleeping on flights, was obeying the pilot's injunction to look out of the window at Reykjavik. At that point, the stewardess delivered a message from Pierre and Margaret Trudeau, inviting us to cocktails and dinner at Sussex Drive that evening. I tried to behave as though this were a normal event, and said I would have to consult with Karen, promptly thumping her in the deltoids and waking her up. Of course we said we would be delighted, but then Karen had a sudden awful thought. "We can't go dressed like this," she said. "We can't go to dinner at the prime minister's in flight clothes." Our bags had been checked through to Toronto.

The sympathetic stewardess heard this and said she would be right back. True to her word, she returned with the solution in hand: she had been instructed to take our measurements. Out came a tape measure — where from I have no idea — and in no time our dimensions were being sent over the airwaves to the prime minister's office. Someone would select clothes for us, we were told, and they would be ready at the store in the Château Laurier. Compliments of the prime minister.

When we arrived in Ottawa, we went straight to the clothing store at the hotel. Karen received a dress with large, colourful flowers all over it, not her at all, but the only thing that came close to fitting, and with only one hour to spare, it would have to do. I helped pin her in with safety pins and then tried on my own outfit — a dazzling combination of beige shirt and beige trousers. I looked like a mushroom, and, together, we looked like a comedy team: Karen, the garden from *Alice in Wonderland*, and Frank, the giant fungus. I don't remember much about the party or the dinner, but I do know that our Wonderland-Fungus clothes were never worn again. Goodwill won out.

Back in Toronto, we found to our amazement we had become minor celebrities. John Fraser, then the dance critic for the *Globe and Mail*, had given Canadians a blow-by-blow account of the competition. This was the beginning of the Kain-Augustyn partnership as a public phenomenon. Our first performance back on home ground was at Ontario Place, a *Swan Lake*. People crowded the grass embankment around the old amphitheatre to get a glimpse of this new phenomenon — us! Whether the partnership, not yet a year old, was ready for all this attention and acclaim, was an open question.

C H A P T E R
6

Now, Which Leg Was It?

Karen and I quickly developed a sort of us-versus-the-rest-of-the-world attitude, as if the rest of the world were barging in on us. There was now tremendous pressure on us both. We had been declared a great partnership by the Canadian press almost before we had begun, and we were ambivalent about the attention. Of course, we wanted it. Then, when it actually arrived on our doorstep, we didn't know how to deal with it. We were so young. What exactly did we have behind us? Nothing in our backgrounds had prepared us for this. Karen's father worked for Westinghouse as a vice-president; my father worked on the shop floor at Stelco. We knew nothing of the media and what media attention could do to your life. Here we were, bombarded with demands for photo sessions, special events, cocktail parties, interviews. It was a circus round that we did our best to

---

As Albrecht, in Giselle.

stumble through. All we were told was to make sure we mentioned the National's season and the major sponsor. That was it. It was an ordeal that took time, energy, and effort – an ordeal that I felt was getting in the way of the work. The last thing you want to do after a long day rehearsing is another interview.

I really never liked doing interviews anyway; the same old questions kept coming up. How does it feel to be a partner? You're the one who stands behind the ballerina, and you don't have much to do, was the implication. You get your one chance, a minute-and-thirty-second solo, to prove that you are good, and that's it. You must feel like you are a second-class citizen on the stage there. That's not very masculine, is it?

I have to say that I rarely felt that way. I was happy and proud to be working with an accomplished ballerina. I was *proud* to present her. After all, most of the time I was a prince, it was my *job*. I never felt I needed to step in front and take that curtain call at the end in order to feel good. I don't think a partnership can work if either the man or the woman needs to be centre stage all the time. When I looked around at the great partnerships in ballet, from Margot Fonteyn and Rudolf Nureyev to Antoinette Sibley and Anthony Dowell to Suzanne Farrell and Peter Martins, I didn't see two people fighting for the limelight. I saw two people working together to make something happen. To me, there was an equality in all of this. There was also something almost mystical, where one plus one made more than two.

There were other perils for me here that Karen did not have to face. She, after all, was a woman. Women are supposed to like ballet. "What made you take up ballet, Frank?" was a typical opening question, loaded with the implication that there was something not quite normal about what I had done. As I've mentioned, when I first started dancing, I was possibly the only person in the universe who didn't know that there was a stigma attached to male ballet dancers. Now, I knew. In the eyes of the media and just about everyone else in the land where hockey ruled, ballet was for girls and women. So I'd have to face these silly questions again and again. It was convoluted, because no one was actually coming right out and saying what they meant. You knew the underlying theme was, What the hell are you, a heterosexual male, doing here in this world of gay men? Always assuming, of course, that you *were* a heterosexual male. Dealing with this without protesting too much, and consequently seeming homophobic, was not easy. I simply did not understand what all the fuss was about. It did not matter to me whether my male friends were gay or straight, I saw people as people. Plus, by the time I was nineteen or twenty, I'd seen male dancers in Russia and Europe who were huge stars, commanding a great deal of respect. They weren't looked down upon because they were ballet dancers. For me, all this illuminated a sickness in our society, which I didn't like, but there was not much I could do about it. The articles about me all seemed to be trying to dispel any confusion there might be out there about my sexuality by making me out to be more heroic and more male, macho rather than creative, tough rather than sensitive. I was angry with many of them, because they made me sound so unlike me. I often came across as a sports jock, when I thought of myself as an aspiring dance artist. I saw nothing in my aspirations to be ashamed of, and I did not need or want to gain "masculinity" by being compared to hockey players.

The publicity Karen and I were getting at this stage belied the fact that our career together was only just beginning, and it almost came crashing to a halt not long after our return from Moscow. In September 1973, we were performing *Giselle* in Winnipeg. Near the beginning of my second-act solo, on the second double cabriole, I

With Karen Kain, in the first act of Giselle.

landed too far back. My knee turned out, and I knew something serious was wrong, because I heard it crack. I completed the variation and the performance without any pain, but I knew something serious had happened. During the curtain calls, Karen could also tell something was wrong because of the distracted look on my face. Back in the hotel, the knee began to swell up. Karen and I sat and watched it get visibly bigger and bigger. "I'm sure it's all right," she said, not very convincingly. "Just put some ice on it. You'll be fine." I iced it for a long time, then went to bed, hoping that by morning it would be miraculously cured. When I woke up, it was worse. I had very little mobility, and the swelling was now enormous. Clearly, I couldn't dance. I left the company and went back to Toronto to get medical advice. The curious thing was that I still didn't have any pain.

In Toronto, I saw Dr. David MacIntosh, an orthopaedic surgeon who was affiliated with the National Ballet. He told me the knee needed to be operated on. I could hardly take in what he was saying to me; all I heard was the word *operation*. Operations could mean the end of a dancer's career. I left his office feeling faint. I went out into the stairwell and sat down on the stairs – for a long time. I was in a state of shock. I decided to get a second opinion, and Dr. John Evans confirmed that an operation was necessary. It turned out to be a very standard job and, as I learned that Evans was a good technician on this kind of thing, I decided he should do it. What had happened was this: over a period of time, I had slowly but surely whittled away at the lateral meniscus, the cartilage between the femur and the tibia. As a result, I had too much rotation in the left knee. When I landed, I'd land in jumps with the knee a little too far back, twisting it. I had been doing it for many years. I had done it once too often.

I was sitting on the bed, in the operating room, before the anaesthetic, when Evans came in. "Now, which leg was it again?" he said.

The black humour was wasted on me. This was no joke. "It's my left knee," I said. "And it's my career." Evans said when he took the cartilage out, it looked like spaghetti. There was the big rupture, but there were other little ruptures all around it. He put it into formaldehyde and showed it to me. "Can I have it?" I asked. "Do you really want it?" He looked at me as if I were crazy. "Well, it is mine," I said. I took it home and kept it for years. Only when it started to swell did I decide the time had come to throw it out.

The doctors said I would be able to dance again in about eight or nine months. That seemed like an eternity, but within a week, there was progress. I was able to walk. The critical thing was that I now knew that I could not injure the knee again, since it would mean the end of dancing. Slowly, gently, but very deliberately, I started working to get back into shape. Today, the operation would be done with an arthroscope, and I would probably have walked out of the hospital, and been spared a four-day stay. I know one dancer who had the same operation done recently, and was back in the studio after only ten days. I spent close to ten months away from the stage. Sports medicine has come a long way in twenty-five years.

Although the doctors had said I could definitely dance again, my worry was whether I would be able to perform as before. Elevation is reduced, flexibility and strength are reduced, the longevity of your career is reduced, and because you are working with bare cartilage on cartilage, you don't have a cushion in there any more. Eventually the cartilage you have will wear away, and you'll have bone on bone. Then you are really finished. Meanwhile, I worked on strength and flexibility and being able to once again fully straighten and bend my knee.

The first thing I had to do was get off my crutches and walk securely without somebody bumping me and knocking me over. Each day, the big question was, How is my walking today? When it was sufficiently stable, I decided I would go away to Europe. Sitting in Toronto, not working, was making me crazy. I could feel depression setting in. The world was busy working, doing interesting things, while I was stuck going to physio, which was the highlight of my day. I didn't want to be in my apartment and I didn't want to go home to my parents. All of my friends were in the company, which was away on tour.

I quickly learned how much I missed what truly had become a family for me, the National Ballet Company. I missed not just the people in the company, but everything we did. From class, to rehearsal, to performance, to travelling, to even the aches and pains. I missed all of it, the whole life. And I missed Karen. I worried who would be able to work with her. Her performances were reduced, because there were few dancers in the company who were tall enough to partner her.

Rudolf called when he heard about the injury. "You should never have let anyone cut you," he said. He never did believe in doctors. "Too late," I said. "It's already done." He thought it should just have been bandaged, and I could have gone on dancing. Rudolf believed in massage — that was his cure for everything. He asked me what I was going to do. When I said that I wanted to go and study in Europe as soon as I could walk normally and steadily, with typical generosity, he offered me the use of his houses in London and France. It was a very kind gesture, and it made going away affordable for me, as I didn't have a lot of cash. I was living on my savings and a little disability insurance.

Even then, I could still only afford to be away for about five weeks. London was my first stop. There, I attended class at the Royal Ballet, with, among others, Anthony Dowell, Antoinette Sibley, Monica Mason, and David Wall. I also visited the Festival Ballet, and various other ballet studios in the city. I went to art galleries, and in the evening the theatre, and, of course, Covent Garden.

Every night I was in the city seeing something. I got a really good sense of what was happening in the dance world. At that time London was considered the centre of ballet, and the standards were noticeably higher than at the National. The Royal Ballet then enjoyed a strong roster of principal dancers, most of whom I saw perform at Covent Garden. I saw Antoinette Sibley and Anthony Dowell in one of their signature pieces, Sir Frederick Ashton's *The Dream*, and Canadian dancer Jennifer Penney dance with Donald MacLeary in *The Sleeping Beauty*. I also went to performances of more contemporary works at Sadler's Wells. Hans van Manen's *Twilight* made a particular impression on me. (Much later in my career, I would get to perform it myself.) I stayed at Rudolf's house in Richmond – a huge place with a library, enormous grounds, a double-car garage, and I don't remember how many bedrooms. I slept in Erik Bruhn's bed, a little single bed, golden white, with an Egyptian look to it. The maid looked after me, made the bed, and cooked my meals. I had never lived in such luxury. I always knew that Rudolf was brilliant and talented, but now I had an idea of just how wealthy he was, too. While I was staying at the house, I met the *Observer* dance critics, Nigel and Maude Gosling, who wrote under the name of Alexander Bland. They came to visit, knowing from Rudolf that I was there alone. It was nice to have the contact, because throughout the whole trip I was quite lonely. I was seeing and learning many things, yet had no one to talk to and share my experiences.

I spent about three weeks in London, then embarked on a lightning tour of companies in Amsterdam, Rome, Stuttgart, and Brussels, before ending up in the south of France. One of Rudolf's recommendations was to study with Marika Besobrasova, in Cannes, which I did for about two weeks. The sun was bright, the beaches were white, the Mediterranean clean. I got some very good training in the morning, followed by some extra coaching sessions, then I had the day to myself. It was relaxing, and at the same time I felt that I was getting better and stronger. I even spent some time in the sun, which I don't really like to do, but I thought it would do me good. I stayed at another of Rudolf's houses, high in the hills north of Monte Carlo, a Spanish-style home with a husband-and-wife team as caretakers. The food was different from anything I was used to; I had real trouble with the lamb's-brain salad. As this white-grey substance lay on the plate, I could see clearly what it was. It was years before I had brain again, but then it was disguised, sautéed in garlic and butter, sprinkled with parsley, and a lot better tasting.

During those five weeks I learned a critical lesson. Suddenly, the world was not as big as I had thought it was. What had seemed remote no longer felt that way. The great institutions of dance, the great teachers I was so in awe of — I trained with them. They became real people to me. These icons, who I thought were untouchable, I touched. I also saw how the traditions had been handed down. It was a very important lesson. On a more personal level, I also learned that I was more resilient than I had thought. I could take a disadvantage and make an advantage out of it. My primary goal was, yes, to dance again. But more than that, I wanted to come back better, with more knowledge both as an individual and as a dancer.

In Europe, I saw an easier, less-regimented way of learning. It seemed to me that artists there were more content and free. A mistake was a mistake, and to be learned from; it wasn't the end of the world. At Maurice Béjart's company, the Ballet of the Twentieth Century at Théâtre de la Homme in Brussels, particularly, there was such a sense of freedom, but also at the Dutch National, I sensed an ease that I hadn't been exposed to. Even at the Royal Ballet, which was in some ways so like the National, the atmosphere was more relaxed. My training had made me hard on myself. In Europe, I learned not to be that way, that a spirit of openness and creativity were every bit as important as rigorous training, and more important than always getting things right. Growth comes with risk, I learned. Failure was just a normal part of learning.

Back in Toronto, I continued working with the company until I was ready to return to the stage. I thought I was ready to perform much earlier than they did, but, I think wisely, they kept me back. I was rehearsing after about four months. By the fifth month, I was doing variations and partnering. I would have relapses, the knee would blow up, and I'd ice it and take it easy for a couple of days. I'd been warned that this would happen; there was scar tissue in there, and it had to break down. I was still haunted by the many stories I had heard of dancers who came back a shadow of their former selves. An injury scares a lot of people – scares the artistic director, scares the coaches, audiences begin to wonder, your partner wonders. Above all, it scares you. I wanted to prove to the world that this was something that actually improved me. At the National, people were sympathetic, but simply unsure of what was going to happen. I was a bright young light on the verge of making a mark. In the first three years I had made an impact – but it *was* only three years.

My first performance back was at the Met in September 1974. It could have been anywhere, but I thought it might as well be there. I danced Bluebird with principal dancer Nadia Potts. There was a little bit of swelling after the performance, but I was dancing again the next day. I was happy with the performance, though I knew it wasn't what I used to do. I wasn't as free as I wanted to be, because I didn't want to throw all cares to the wind. It wasn't an ideal way to perform, but I needed to be cautious. Everyone was very pleased, including Rudolf, and that mattered a great deal to me. I had proved to myself, to my colleagues, and to a very important audience that I was physically healthy. Mentally, I was a different person. I was a little more analytical in my approach to work and I resented the fact that I wasn't impervious to injury. I had never thought that a serious career-threatening injury would ever get me, but it happened when I was only twenty-one. Now, after almost a year away from dancing, it would never be totally out of my mind.

7

A Prince for a Princess

A partnership in the world of classical ballet is very much give-and-take. It's not one dancer trying to be better than the other, or one overshadowing the other, but very much two people facing the audience together. There is a built-in difficulty here. Most classical ballets are constructed around the ballerina, who is usually the focus of the story. That can be a pitfall for the ballerina, who can very easily begin to think that the whole world revolves around her. It can also be a pitfall for the male dancer, who can begin to feel used if his ballerina doesn't recognize the value of a good partner. The male dancer has to present the ballerina, showing her off for the world to see, while at the same time exuding a sense of security and confidence. It doesn't work if he tries to dominate the ballerina, and it doesn't work if, as is more commonly the case, she tries to dominate him.

With Karen, as Prince and Princess, in The Sleeping Beauty.

Finding a good partnership changes your life – forever. For Karen and me, it felt as if we had been given a gift. I had never felt anything like it before, and haven't since, but for those seven or eight years, when the partnership with Karen was at its height, I felt that we had been blessed. Very few dancers are given the luxury of a good partnership. That we had this, and had it so early in our careers, was very rare. I knew it was special – just how special was something that I only very much later came to appreciate. All I knew then was that what we were doing together was great.

Karen is a very giving person and a very giving dancer. When we danced together, I never felt that she was dancing for herself or on her own. I always felt that she never forgot I was there. In any moment, she would be trying to communicate with me, as I would be with her. It was a constant exchange on stage, a connective thread. I've danced with ballerinas with whom I knew that certain passages would go by, and they'd be concentrating so much on their own steps that they would ignore me. Right then, in the rehearsal, I knew that there was a big gap and that there would not be any communication in the performance. This never happened with Karen. As a result, we were able to project an image of two people dancing as one. I don't think that on any conscious level we knew what we were doing. It is hard to say how much of this organic unity came from our personal relationship. We were partners before we were lovers. I think it may have worked the other way. We felt that what we had together as dancers was such a natural thing, why not take it one step further? If it worked for us in dance, it should work for us in our personal lives. Later, we were to find that what serves you well in one area of your life doesn't necessarily work well in other areas. But that was later.

At that time, and through to about 1980, my career centred around my partnership with Karen. We became, if not quite household names, then at least well enough known in the dance world that audiences would call the box office asking when we were dancing.

Tickets for our performances were usually sold out. The Kain and Augustyn partnership was one of the National Ballet's prime draws, which gave us the nickname of the "Gold Dust Twins." What people came to see was a partnership that worked.

In some ways, it was easier being part of something that worked than trying to figure out, some twenty years on, *why* it worked. A few things are obvious. For a start, our personalities blended. Karen worked with great attack, almost to the point of desperation. With her, there was a burning need and desire to dance. I found that very attractive, that total sense of life going into the dance. I complemented her in the sense that I also found great joy in dancing and had a similar huge desire to explore, although I was less attacking and driven than she. There was the added benefit that we looked good together – both tall and dark, with similar proportions and a similar sense of line. Matching physicality and attitude are important, and these we had. We also had good training, the same kind of musicality, and seemed to have a facility for speaking as easily in dance as in words. Our early reputations were made on the great classics of nineteenth-century ballet, among them *Giselle* and *Swan Lake*.

These ballets could all be great scenarios for *This Hour Has 22 Minutes*. They are ripe for satire. Take *Giselle*. A young peasant girl falls in love with a man that she does not know is a) a prince and b) engaged to someone else. When she finds out, depending on how the ballet is interpreted, she either kills herself or dies of heart failure. Then, in the second act, as a spirit, she saves her lover from a group of mad female spirits – all jilted women – who set out to wreak revenge on him. A feminist interpretation of the ballet is not far off the mark: this is a killer body of women, out to get the bad guy. True love, however, wins out in the end, and the prince survives. Stated this baldly, it all sounds very silly. But look again: how silly is it to fall in love, and then be hurt and rejected? And how silly is it that, after someone dies, you feel the presence of a person you have loved? How

Above: Rehearsing with Karen, at the Bolshoi.

Below: Daily class, with Karen. The intensity is there on our faces.

silly is it to believe in the spirit world? If you believe in levels of life and death, as I do, then all of a sudden the story becomes quite believable.

In the beginning, dancing was less of a problem than acting. We had never been taught much about acting. In school, we had theatre-arts classes, where we were given scenarios that we had to act out, but we were never taught anything specific about communicating emotion. How do you show emotion on your face in a way that does not look like bad silent-film acting? How do you do this when your bunions are sore, and your back is sore, and you think you've wrenched your knee? None of this was ever touched upon. So much attention was concentrated on the number-one priority of acquiring the skills to dance that we barely scratched the surface on how to present character. At first I found acting difficult, a difficulty not eased by the fact that all the classic male roles seemed to be princes. Is there any way to make a prince believable or interesting? Yet, if he isn't believable or interesting, what does that do to the ballet? *Giselle*, like all the nineteenth-century classics, is very much focussed on the ballerina. That said, the stronger and more convincing the male role can be, the more potent the performance.

In *Giselle*, I viewed the character of Albrecht as being not very serious at all – at the beginning. He had seen Giselle from a distance, and for him it was a conquest game. But the closer he got to her, the more he came to like her. Through the first act, I tried to show him falling more in love with her. It's all a little unreal, but it is essential to make it believable and to do that, you yourself have to believe in it. Otherwise, it will come across to the audience as fake. To make it work for me, I invented a whole back story for the ballet: I'd watched Giselle for days in the village, I told myself, and had planned the whole thing. I had sent my servant Wilfrid out to steal or buy peasant clothes for me from another village. Albrecht was young and footloose.

He had decided to amuse himself, and got in a little deeper than he might have wanted.

We were blessed with Sir Peter Wright's version of the ballet, originally staged for the Stuttgart Ballet, which has to be one the more intelligent. Here, the relationship between Albrecht and Giselle is central, with the character roles of Giselle's mother, and her other suitor, Hilarion, limited to what is necessary to carry along the plot. The only thing that bothered me with this version was the lack of clarity on how Giselle died. Does she stab herself, die of a weak heart, or die of madness? It's always called the "mad scene," but I don't think she actually goes mad. Karen, like most ballerinas, played Giselle as an innocent. When the truth was revealed, that Albrecht was a prince engaged to marry another woman of his own rank, Karen played it as devastating emotional blow, such a blow that nothing else mattered in her life. She was broken-hearted. In her view, Giselle died of sadness.

Peter Wright came over from England for a brief period to work with us. He was articulate and precise, about both character and movement. He wanted no extraneous movement. Everything had to be very focussed. Giselle was to hold her head forward, with arching neck and back, a hard posture to hold and exactly what we were trained not to do. Wright was as much a stage director as a choreographer, and he gave me good dramatic direction. For Giselle's mad scene, he made me think about what the prince was going through. He has been exposed, he has a rival there whom he would like to kill, and above everything he is confused about what is happening to Giselle. This all helped me make Albrecht real — just in case anyone in the audience should be paying any attention to him at that point, when he's hardly the focus of dramatic attention.

Karen and I performed *Giselle* when we were asked to dance in the Soviet Union in 1977. It was an honour rarely accorded to dancers from the West, and we were thrilled. Our tour comprised Moscow,

Kiev, Tallinn, and Vilnius, starting at the Bolshoi in Moscow. We began by learning the Bolshoi version of the ballet, and were told that, once we had learned their choreography, we'd be set. We soon found out that this was part of the imperial arrogance of the Bolshoi. In Kiev they had a different version. In fact, all the companies turned out to have different versions. That did not stop the Bolshoi saying their version was the definitive version, the version that everybody else did. They believed that anyone who didn't do their version was both a fool and not politically correct — which may be two different ways of saying the same thing.

In one production of the Bolshoi version, in a rehearsal of the entrance of Albrecht in the second act, I came on with the music and looked back to find a rather crumpled individual following me. It was Wilfrid, my servant from the first act. This was not how we did the ballet. In the National's version, he does not appear at all in the second act. I thought it was the funniest thing in the world, and had a hard time trying not to laugh. I asked that he not accompany me, because to me it was comical, particularly with the way he did it — all mournful, with drooping shoulders, like something out of a D. W. Griffith melodrama. Our Russian Wilfrid was not at all upset about this. In fact, he was delighted not to be there. It meant he could leave early after the first act and head for the bar.

This second trip to the old Soviet Union was so different from the first. I was happy that it wasn't a competition, and this time I wasn't nervous at all. In every way, the trip was more comfortable, although I don't think you ever really recapture the excitement and interest of seeing new places for the first time. We were in a better hotel, we had personal interpreters, the food was better, and — an even bigger bonus — there was enough of it. Our performances were sold out and we had a very good reception, finding that people remembered us from the competition four years earlier. We seemed to capture the hearts of the Russian audiences, who were much warmer than Canadian audiences. In a strange way, they seemed more like American audiences than the reserved Canadians. The applause was louder and it went on and on, a healthy "we like you and we're going to show you" feeling.

Our performances were as good as they could be, given that we were in a foreign country, with new people around us, and having to rehearse very quickly. Dancing with Karen was, of course, easy. Fitting in with the rest of the production was trickier, and took more work. All the *mise en scène* work had to be adjusted, although our pas de deux choreography remained as it was for the National version. There were mishaps, of course. At the Bolshoi, we made an entrance too early in the first act, and had to extricate ourselves from the corps de ballet, then wait onstage for our cue. Then Karen fell in the mad scene, getting splinters in her hand and her behind. She survived this with grace, endearing herself to the audience, and the second act went without mishap. When the curtain came down, the generous Bolshoi audience gave us a nine-minute standing ovation and six curtain calls.

The trip was a chance to get to know some of the Soviet dancers, and it confirmed for me what I always suspected. Dancers were dancers were dancers. All over the world they seem to be the same. Communist or capitalist, we have the same concerns, the same complaints, the same common ground. Globally, there is a hunger for new work and good leadership. Technique and interpretation are always fascinating for all dancers, things as simple as why you do pointe-tendu first in class rather than a plié. On a practical level, there is the obsession with gear, particularly footwear — what shoes you wear, how you break your shoes in — and injuries. There is always talk of injuries and how to treat them. Another common bond is complaining. We are all good complainers — about our companies, artistic directors, and choreographers.

Many of the Russian dancers understood and spoke English, and class was in French, so it wasn't difficult to get along. Looking at how they lived, it was clear that these were privileged people. Dancers in the old Soviet Union were really respected. They had a good life. They had first dibs on things that weren't readily available to everyone. To get a car, they didn't have to wait in line as long. They could get better apartments. The food in the Bolshoi canteen was better than you could get anywhere else in the city. There was the good hospital and the bad hospital, and dancers got to go to the good hospital. They were stars, and were treated as such. That said, there was still very little available for them in the way of consumer goods, and, like everyone else, they depended on a flourishing black market. We went to GUM, the Moscow department store, and saw how little was there. Much later, in 1992, I went back to Moscow. By then, if you had money, you could buy anything. Gucci shoes had come to GUM.

Karen and I did many, many other performances of *Giselle*, but one of them stands out in my mind. We were in Fredericton, of all places, on a fairly small stage, one of those where the orchestra pit is actually underneath the stage. There was a little hole downstage centre, where George Crum, the conductor, could pop his head up, see the dancers, and then duck back down to the orchestra. We'd look at George in the rehearsal, and he'd resemble a bobbing seal. It was not a particularly auspicious start.

The performance began, and from the very beginning everything was so right. The steps flowed and seemed effortless. Karen and I were absolutely in unison, more so than ever before. Fredericton doesn't often give standing ovations, but after this performance, they did. Our coaches came backstage with tears in their eyes, which was highly unusual — they've seen the ballet so often, and they've even seen *you* do it more times than they care to count. Some of the other dancers were crying. Karen and I looked at each other and said, What happened? What happened? To this day, I can hardly remember what we did, in terms of how many pirouettes I did, or how well Karen did her variations, or how well the lifts went. What I remember was this amazing feeling that someone else was doing this for me. It was almost as if an outside force came down and did it for us. Karen and I talked about it after the performance. We both had the same feeling, that we weren't really doing this, that we weren't really ourselves. Neither of us will ever forget it. If only I knew the key, the secret. We gave many good, maybe even great, performances, but I can count on the fingers of one hand the performances I felt *that* good about.

This was the partnership at its very best. Yet when I try to define what we had further, it becomes almost impossible to pin down. First and foremost, we were friends, and being friends makes working with someone a lot easier. It frees you to be more open and more honest, when you know that the person opposite you likes you or loves you. Trust was also very important, perhaps the single most important thing. I loved Karen, liked her, trusted her, and accepted her idiosyncrasies — as she did mine. Our temperaments sometimes dovetailed, but there were also ways in which they sometimes clashed. Karen's drive for perfection was complemented by my more easy-going attitude. That difference could both help us and cause problems. I was always more patient than Karen. If I saw something that didn't work, I wouldn't beat myself up about it. I would take a step back, go off and do something else, then come back to the problem, hopefully with renewed strength and energy. It was an approach that I think sometimes made Karen nervous and anxious. Other times, I think it calmed her down. There were occasions when we would get into some pretty intense battles about how to do something; one thing we did have in common was that we were both pretty bull-headed. We survived our differences through a common desire to be as good as we possibly could be and through a common bond of humour. Karen and I knew how to laugh together, and I am a firm believer that you become stronger when you know someone understands laughter with you. We also heard music in the same way. It was a bonus that we were trained at the same school. I think we were equally strong in being able to communicate with an audience and to reach past the footlights. We did not suffer from the kind of imbalance here that can so easily ruin a potential partnership.

You can list all these things – liking, trust, temperamental compatibility, good training, humour, talent, a well-matched look, a similar musicality – much as if they were a recipe. What is missing in this list is the one thing that everyone says is needed for great partnerships and which everyone likes to call chemistry, for want of any better, more descriptive, word. "Chemistry" was something I think we had, at least in the beginning. I think you can make a partnership work with the right combination of the individual ingredients and through sheer mastery of the craft. But it never speaks with as loud a voice as natural chemistry. That, we were blessed with.

One of the great tests of a partnership in classical ballet is *Swan Lake*, which we danced often during our career together. Given the nature of the National's production, which had been radically re-worked by Erik Bruhn, dancer-turned-choreographer, the challenges it presented were not just those relating to partnership. Character matters in this ballet, and the character challenges are very different for the Prince and Odette/Odile. For Karen, it was a glorious role, the prized and most demanding ballerina role in the repertoire. I think what she had as Odette was an innocence and delicateness, a mystical quality. In a lot of ways, she resembled Natalia Makarova. Their approaches to the role were similar, with the same feeling – of a creature who would instantly fly away if so much as a pebble dropped on the water. The Black Swan was something Karen had to work on more. I think the fiery nature didn't come naturally to her,

With Karen, the White Swan pas de deux from Swan Lake.

With Karen, the Black Swan pas de deux.

but she persisted. As for me, the role of the Prince started out as a psychological struggle. Later, it became a nightmare.

Male dancers have mixed feelings about *Swan Lake*. Audiences adore the ballet, the music is glorious, and there is so much good dancing in it. However, if you are playing the Prince, early on in the ballet most of that good dancing seems reserved for someone else. Peter Martins, of New York City Ballet, has said that he absolutely hated dancing *Swan Lake* because it isn't until midway through the third act that the Prince really gets anything significant to do. Up to that point his main role, in most versions of the ballet, is to stand around and be indecisive. Erik Bruhn had tried to fix this problem by making the Prince much more the focus of the ballet. He gave him a murderously difficult solo at the end of Act I, which looked sensational on his own body, but was a whole lot harder for the rest of us to accomplish. Many dancers changed the steps to make it look good on them. I tried to be as true to the choreography as possible.

I felt a great responsibility toward making the ballet work. Even though there is a limit to the Prince's dancing, *Swan Lake* is only as good as the Prince, because, if he botches up the story in the first place, he can ruin the overall impact. He needs to carry the bulk of the first act, and there is nothing that the Swan Queen can do to lift the performance back up if he hasn't done his job. Erik Bruhn's version, which the National no longer performs, is much darker than most productions, and not without its share of misogyny. The Prince is a very confused young man, and there are strong hints that his confusion has a lot to do with his mother. Instead of the usual male Von Rothbart evil-magician character, Erik had a female, evil Black Queen Mother. When the National was first mounting the production, Grant Strate, who was then resident choreographer with the National, tried to pin Erik down on the reason why he wanted the Von Rothbart character to be female, and how she was to be characterized.

A curtain call at the Metropolitan in New York.

Grant is a very forthright character, and he's very good at getting to the heart of the matter, but he couldn't get a satisfactory answer out of Erik. So the production had gone ahead, with several passages unclarified. It was an unspoken assumption that the ballet represented Erik's less-than-happy relationship with his mother.

When I first did the ballet, I was only vaguely aware of all this. I thought it was a wonderfully constructed ballet, especially at the end, where the Prince throws himself in the lake and Odette is left alone. It was very poignant. Musically, it was beautiful. Combining the first and second and third and fourth acts contributed immensely to the flow. However, although Erik gave both more dramatic prominence and more dancing to the Prince, the character was still underdeveloped. I think that's why I had to fight with it so much. I think we all saw what Erik had tried to do, but it never really worked. If you are going to put the focus on the Prince, rather than the Swan, then really flesh out the character. A good idea, perhaps, but a bad script.

My prime goal early on was just to learn it, get through it, and – my big ambition in all roles – not fall over. After I'd managed that a few times, I got more and more involved in trying to understand the complexities. I struggled with it for many years, spending more time agonizing over it than any other role. Erik Bruhn had put so much of himself into the character, understanding *Swan Lake* became part and parcel of understanding Erik Bruhn, who was notoriously enigmatic. Even when I later spent more time with him, Erik remained opaque to me. I always had the feeling that he never really wanted anyone to know who he was.

All my agonizing over the character of the Prince apparently did not detract from our performances. This was one ballet we always sold out, and reviews for our performances were consistently good, even if critics continued to carp about the Freudian tones of the production. Again, as with *Giselle*, one performance stands out in my mind. It was in Toronto, to mark the hundredth anniversary of the first performance of the ballet, and although we had done it many, many times before, it had never felt like this. Once again, we were carried through almost as if we ourselves were not doing it. I don't want to take this too far, but it was almost spiritual in its intensity. So often, with Karen, it was.

Dreams and Nightmares

When, in 1976, I first saw my name on the bulletin board, cast as James in *La Sylphide*, I was totally surprised. I had assumed the role would only go to an older dancer. When I entered the company, six years earlier, I thought I had arrived. This was a second symbol of my arrival: the opportunity to perform the first ballet I had ever seen, the one that had set me on the path to becoming a dancer.

La Sylphide is a nineteenth-century morality play, the moral of which comes down to: beware of marriage outside the group. James, the hero — for once in a nineteenth-century ballet, the central character is a man — is engaged to Effie. But he sees an otherwordly spirit, and falls in love with her. That's when the trouble begins. For me, this ballet was not at all hard to believe in. I believe we have spirits, and that our bodies are guided by them. All I had to do was

---

As Colas, in La Fille Mal Gardée.

My dream role, as James in La Sylphide. *With Linda Maybarduk as Effie.*

imagine what it was like to be in love with a very attractive earthly creature, Effie, who would make a wonderful wife, and yet be still wondering if there were something else. The sylph becomes a symbol of this yearning, and James deserts Effie and goes in pursuit of her. Of course, it all ends badly. Madge, the witch, has James tempt the sylph with a magic scarf that symbolizes her death. He shows the sylph the scarf, and she is entranced by it. He teases her, then finally gives it to her, and she dies. James is left without her. He is also left without Effie, who has married another man from the village. There is no hope for him, and he welcomes his own death. The witch kills him and, in her glory at the end of the ballet, laughs as she stands over his dead body.

It's dark, dark story. A children's tale, but very much in the Grimm tradition. Even as a twelve-year-old, I understood the relationships between everyone in this ballet. I understood his death; I understood the triumph of the witch. I understood why he fell in love with this incredible sylph – Lois Smith, in the version I saw – who was such a light, delicate, incredibly ghostlike creature. Plus, for a small boy to look at a ballet like this and see the man as the central character of the drama, that was something. If *Swan Lake* had been the first ballet I ever saw, would I have enjoyed it as much? Would it have given me the desire to become a dancer?

I remember thinking, as the curtain went up before my first performance, that I could not perform the ballet and keep my memory of Earl Kraul and Lois Smith. I had to look at it as my own, as having absolutely no past for me. If I for one moment remembered the way they had danced, and the effect it had on me, my nerves would have got the better of me. This was to be my performance. This decided, it went well, and I was happy with it. Later, I danced James with the Italian ballerina Carla Fracci, who was generally agreed to be the twentieth century's greatest interpreter of the sylph. But my strongest memory of the ballet is not of the first time I danced it, or even of Carla Fracci, extraordinary though she was. It is of a memorable weekend in 1976, when I did five consecutive performances with the National in Toronto.

After the first of these, I wasn't feeling well, and my coaches, Joanne Nisbet and David Scott, took me home with them, made me a hot toddy, and put me to bed. I had an evening performance to do the next day. So I dragged myself out of bed the next morning and set off for the theatre. When I arrived there, I was told that everyone, including Fernando Bujones, who had flown in from American Ballet Theatre in New York to do the ballet, was sick. There was no one to do the matinee. The other sick dancers had all had the good sense to stay home. I was there, a captive. Could I do both performances? I had a fever, so the doctor came in and looked at me. "I don't know how I'm going to do this," I said. "Just take these pills," he replied. I was hesitant, but I took the pills, and started to feel much, much better. I did the matinee, and after the show I rested at the theatre, waiting for my scheduled evening performance. Shortly before I was due to go on, the doctor came in again with more little magic pills. I took a few and soon felt great again. Somehow, I got through. I'd done an evening performance, then the matinee, then another evening – all sick.

My coaches took me home again, and I spent a very bad night, aching all over, with a huge fever. The next day, it was back to the theatre again for another two performances. That third day, I welcomed the doctor. There was no hesitation now. "Please," I said, "I'll take the pills. Just give me the pills." I did five performances in three days. They were supposed to be split among three different dancers, but I did them all. Every single one. This was my dream ballet and it had turned into a nightmare. But did I enjoy it? I loved it. This was my ballet. I had put a lot of work into James, and felt that it had paid off. To this day, I don't know what was in those pills.

~∼

My early years with the company were characterized by unsettled times in management. As dancers, we weren't privy to what was going on; in those days it was not considered our business. Our job then was to follow orders, to do what we were told. But by 1974, we knew something was badly wrong. We knew that Betty and Celia had not been getting along, and it seemed as if the structure was crumbling. I could feel the uncertainty, and it made me apprehensive. Betty certainly felt that it was time for a change, and that Celia should be out. They were both opinionated women, and highly critical of each other at that time.

Most of us had a fierce loyalty to Celia Franca. I certainly did. In 1972, David Haber, an arts administrator, had been appointed co-artistic director, and he and Celia were expected to run the company together. Then, abruptly, Celia was no longer there, leaving David to run things on his own. We were all concerned and we felt abandoned. The artistic operation of the company was left up to ballet masters and mistresses. We needed an artistic director. We needed the artistic stimulus. I certainly felt that, with Celia, my career was being guided, and there was a protection in this. I believed in Celia: she was a keen and astute artist, with very good taste.

Celia Franca in many ways *was* the National Ballet for me. She was our security blanket, our fearless leader. She had taught us most of what we knew – how to be professional, how to portray works with appropriate style. She gave us our good work ethic. With every class, rehearsal, and performance, there was a concentration level we were expected to achieve. Celia gave us our sense of theatricality. She was always theatrical, and if she had not chosen to be a dancer, she would have made a great stage director. She was also a perceptive and very opinionated individual. From her I learned it was okay to have strong opinions, and that the right thing to do was to follow your instincts and to do what you believed in. In some ways that wasn't exactly what she expected of us; she operated as a dictator who didn't want independent minds, at least not within her brood of dancers. But the lessons you learn from someone's behaviour are not always the lessons they would have you learn.

With Celia gone, the dancers had lost their mother figure. David Haber outlasted Celia by only a few months. He could have made a wonderful general manager for the company, if there had also been an artistic director. You could really sense that he loved the company, and that he understood and sympathized with the dancers, which is not always true with a general manager. They are usually accountant types, for whom numbers mean everything, but he was different.

Things settled down when our new artistic director, Alexander Grant, arrived on the scene in July 1976. Alexander Grant was a funny, gregarious, approachable man, who immediately put everyone at ease. Now we felt we had an artistic director with a solid reputation. Alexander had been a character dancer without equal in the Royal Ballet, a man on whom Sir Frederick Ashton had built many great comedic roles. As an artist he had more than proved his worth, plus he had directed the Royal Ballet's small touring troupe, Ballet for All, so we knew that he had some experience running a company. Alexander was a man with the theatre in his bones. He knew what it was to be a dancer, and throughout his stay at the National his humanity shone through. He cared for us, as dancers. There were those who thought he cared too much, that he was not ruthless enough to run a company. I didn't see it that way. Over the seven years he was with us, I thought he did well. I was sorry for the messy way it turned out at the end, but that's getting ahead of the story. At the beginning, everything was full of hope and promise.

Alexander's approach to running a company could not have been more different than Celia's. Celia had been a matriarch surrounded by her children. Alexander came in with what was then a novel concept at the National: everyone is an adult. I may be the artistic director, but the one thing I definitely am not is your mother or father. I make the decisions, you do the work, yes. How you interpret, that is your decision, and I'll allow you a certain freedom there. Some people saw this as weakness. Personally, I loved the change. He was giving everyone the benefit of the doubt, giving the members of the company the freedom to develop their own artistry.

His early years were vibrant. Alexander looked at the talent in the company, and brought in work to complement that talent. As a close friend of Sir Frederick Ashton, he had access to some of the greatest choreographic works of the twentieth century. One of the pieces he brought in for us was one of my all-time favourite ballets, Sir Fred's *La Fille Mal Gardée.* I had seen the first-act pas de deux at the Moscow competition, but I had never seen the whole ballet. It was like reading a great script. Fun, difficult, but so brilliant: and when you are working on anything brilliant you automatically rise to the occasion. There is such a will to master it well and do justice to it.

It was also a work that was almost perfect for Karen and myself at that stage in our careers. To do it well, you have to be young in spirit and have good comedic timing. It is almost impossible to destroy this ballet in performance, it is so well constructed, but to do it really well, you need these things, along with a pretty strong technique and a temperament that is not fazed by lots of business with props. We both really enjoyed that ballet — we had the same sense of humour, and we could really show off how good our comedic timing was. It showed another side of us.

Dancer Georgina Parkinson came to Toronto to teach us the work. Then Sir Fred came over to coach in the final few days prior to opening night to give the finishing touches. We worked well with him, and although he had a few corrections to make, they amounted to very little in the end. Most of the time he would sit there quietly in the studio, very still, a cigarette drooping from his lips. Then, all of a

Above: The terrifying ribbons of La Fille Mal Gardée.

Below: Watching a rehearsal of La Fille Mal Gardée: *Sir Frederick Ashton, foreground;*
Michael Sommes, centre; Alexander Grant, right; and David Scott, standing.

sudden, he'd stand up, or he'd make a gesture, and the entire studio would fall into silence because he had *moved*. The great man had moved. Then he would say, in a very quiet voice, with his arthritic fingers holding the cigarette, "It should be more like this." The coaches would then rush around to make sure everyone knew what God had said. At one point, he stood up again, and the entire studio fell into silence. He took his time – you could have heard a pin drop. Then, all of a sudden, he danced. This old man, with a cigarette in his hand, was doing high kicks, and turning. He had transformed into the character he was demonstrating. This craggy old man was suddenly very beautiful, lithe and graceful. Sir Frederick Ashton, a man in his seventies, kicking and almost hitting his nose. Then he sat back down, and was rock-still again.

"I shouldn't be doing that," he said to Alexander.

"I wish you'd do more of it," Alexander boomed back. Just having Sir Fred there was exhilarating for us. I think he was happy to be there, too. Alexander Grant was elated through it all, because his friend was there for him.

On opening night, at the final moment prior to the curtain going up, Karen and I were trying a few moves on stage, just to get that last feel of each other. Ashton was there, and came over to me. "Don't worry about a thing," he said. "It's going to be great." They were the usual cheerleading words of encouragement, but they did little to calm my nerves. He then went to Karen and said something to her, and she turned away from him, and began to cry. He saw this, and went back to her to ask what was wrong. "I know I'm big," she said. "I know I'm too big." She had heard of his preference for small dancers in the role. "What on earth are you talking about?" he asked. Karen thought Ashton had said, "I wish you would shrink." What he had actually said was "I wish I had a drink." He started laughing, she started laughing, I started laughing. It was such a funny thing for her to get upset at. All our nerves were so strung out.

The audience loved the ballet. Everything worked – and there was a lot to make work in that ballet. There is the nightmare of the cat's-cradle pas de deux. Lise and Colas, the young lovers, perform a pas de deux with ribbons, in which they make a cat's cradle. It is a big moment in the ballet, when the cat's cradle is revealed, a moment when audiences gasp with pleasure, but you could never, ever, be sure that it was going to turn out. There were so many things that could go wrong. You could tie the knot wrong, or get the ribbons caught trying to pull them over your shoulders. Usually, it would be wider at one end than the other. It was very scary. You end up not thinking of posture, technique, or anything else at all, except just tie the damn ribbon so that it doesn't come apart. You're clammy, sweaty, and you've got these two ends of a ribbon, which you have to tie properly. If you don't, the whole thing is gone. It's like sitting on the couch, tying your shoelace, with three thousand people watching you while you're doing it.

Then there was the Colas bottle solo. He has to perform this very energetic solo in between two bottles that are placed on stage in full sight of the audience. All you think about while doing this is "Please, God, don't let me knock a bottle over." I kept thinking, if only I could do my double attitude turns without the bottles there, it would be so much easier. But no, the whole point is that you have to do them around the bottles, that's what makes it interesting. Interesting for the audience, maybe. There is so much *stuff* in this ballet that, if you don't approach it in the right frame of mind, it gets in your way.

With *Fille* there were performances that just clicked, when the acting was easier and the timing for the jokes was bang on. I found it so interesting to do comedy. You don't flow through the myriad emotions in *Fille* that you do in the tragedies that are the major part of the classical repertoire, but what was fabulous, what was really interesting, was making it work. What mattered was delivering a "punchline" at exactly the right time, with exactly the right feeling, with exactly the right volume, and that's very hard to do in dance. It's very hard to do, period. It was most fun with Karen, because we knew how to make it work, just waiting for the right moment to give that look, or to make that gesture, or to embellish a little bit of expression. We are really talking about milliseconds of timing here. For me, *Fille* was every bit the accomplishment that any of the great dramas were. There was a different kind of satisfaction to it – which was none the less real or intense. It's a great ballet, so full of character and humanity. That was Ashton's great strength – his humanity. He loved people and he loved to be able to tell stories.

Our performances of the ballet were always enhanced when Alexander Grant performed the role he had created: Alain, the rich simpleton who is in love not with the heroine, Lise, whom he is supposed to marry, but with his umbrella. I wish I had seen Alexander when he was younger, for he lifted the ballet to another level. Alexander didn't play for the laugh, but did it more as a clown would do it, making you feel for him while you were laughing at his misfortunes. He brought out the sadness of it all, moving beyond caricature to make the ballet very bittersweet. When we did it with him, he was really past doing the role, but he was such a stage animal that he was determined to go on. He loved every minute of it, despite the fact that he already had problems with a degenerating hip. I felt for him after the performances, when he would be crippled for days. Eventually, like so many dancers, he got a hip replacement. In fact, he has now had two of them.

~~~

All through these adventures, my mother and father were keeping a keen eye on my career. My visits home were now rare. My parents would come in from Hamilton to see our performances at the

O'Keefe Centre, visit backstage afterwards, and delight in meeting the dancers. They were very proud of me and my success, although that success did nothing to convince my father that I'd made a good choice of career. He still felt that I shouldn't be dancing, that I should find something more secure for myself – something more respectable, like accounting. If I had to dance, he had definite opinions about what I should be dancing, how much I should be paid, and what I should be wearing both on and off stage. He always thought I should wear a tie, and he particularly liked how I looked in *Don Quixote*, probably the only role in classical ballet where a tie is part of the man's costume. My mother would be interested in when and where reviews could be found, and, like many a mother, she kept a file of clippings. I never cared that much myself about the reviews, but I was glad that my parents were happy and proud.

Their pride increased when, in 1979, I received the Order of Canada. I could take only one guest with me to the ceremony in Ottawa, so I asked my brother, Peter, to accompany me. He was still living at home, which he does to this day, and working at McMaster University as a computer draughtsman. Peter and I had been so close as children, but over the years, as my visits home became less frequent, we had drifted apart. Peter had been my best friend, and I wanted him in Ottawa, to share in the award.

I had another reason for asking him to come. For several years, I had noticed that something was not quite right with the way Peter moved. I have a trained eye for body language. What people do with their bodies is very telling, and I can almost predict what people are going to say prior to their saying it by watching how they move. I know instantly if someone has an injury by watching them walk, and my brother appeared to me to be moving abnormally. I noticed that, if he reached for something at the table, he would do it clumsily. He would stand in an awkward, almost off-balance way. Every time I asked if he was all right, he said he was fine, but I knew that something was wrong. It was in Ottawa, just after the ceremony, that I found out how serious the problem was.

We were in our hotel room, and I asked him to take off his shirt. I wanted to check his muscles. I took off my shirt, and we stood together in front of the hotel mirror. To my horror, he had bruises all the way down his spine, his deltoids were almost completely disintegrated, and areas of his chest and rib muscles were wasted. I stood, with my youthful, developed dancer's body, next to my brother, who was only one year older than me, but had the wizened shape of a much older man. All I could say was, "Peter, there is something very wrong." As we stood there, looking in that mirror, Peter wasn't angry with me, as he might well have been. He was accepting. Which, when I thought about it later, was so much more in his character. He was the cautious one, the one who, unlike me, would not impulsively spend the money we earned on our paper route. The cautious one, who wouldn't ride his bike down the hill at breakneck speed. The dutiful one, who had stayed home to care for our parents. Where I argued and challenged, Peter placated and smoothed. He was the solid one, the one with his feet on the ground. I always felt I was more in the sky than Peter. He was the realist. We spent a long time that night, with the lights out, talking.

On his return home, Peter was examined by doctors in Hamilton, but a clear diagnosis was not established. Some doctors thought the muscle weakness could be a form of muscular dystrophy. Others were not so sure. In February the following year, he was admitted to Toronto General Hospital for two weeks for more tests. He was told he had polymyositis, a muscle illness similar to muscular dystrophy. Peter was worried – not knowing if there was any therapy that could help. The drug prednisone brought some improvement, and he began to feel better. He carried on with his life as before, taking courses in French, music, and painting, working at McMaster University, and living at home with our parents. For him, this was not hard – he was always much more understanding of them than I was. He could never understand how I could be so critical and fight so hard over so much with my father. To him, this wasn't necessary. Change what you can, accept what you can't, was his attitude. That is what he has done in his life, and to me he is a kind of saint.

It was only very much later, in 1999, that his diagnosis was revised – after yet more tests – to limb-girdle muscular dystrophy, which is an adult form of muscular weakness. It turns out that the disease is inherited. Which gave me something to think about. It could have been me.

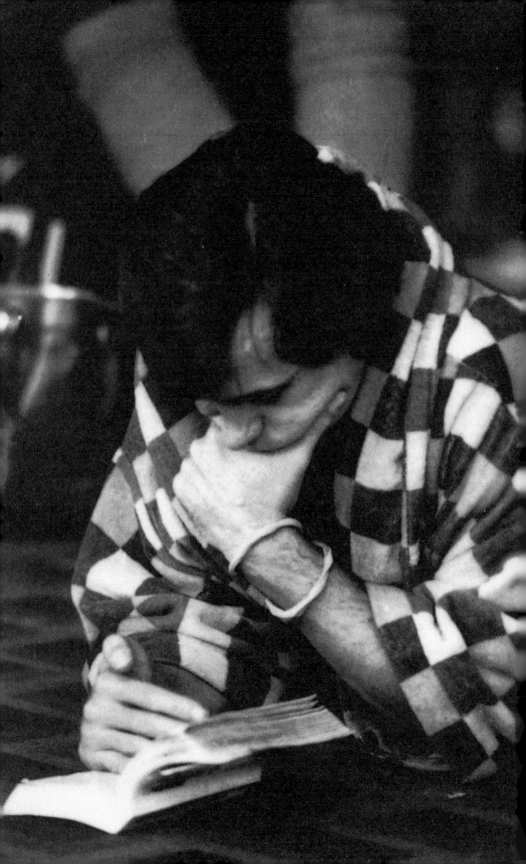

On the Road

There were times during those early years with the company that we seemed to be constantly on the road. Touring was both good and bad. It was wonderful because you packed your suitcase, locked up your apartment, leaving all your cares and worries behind you, and away you went. No cooking, no cleaning, no dishes — that was a definite advantage, being able to concentrate more on the adventures ahead. But travelling also had its difficulties: the constant daily round of buses, hotels, checking in, checking out, always moving, never being rooted in one place. Days spent doing class on stage in strange theatres, followed by rehearsals and performance. Then, after the performance, the big focus was finding a place to eat. We were pretty hungry when we finished at around midnight, when very little was open, and often the best you could do was a pizza.

Relieving the tedium of touring.

Above: Backstage on the road, Alexander Grant in serious
conversation with Charles Kirby.
Below: I had finally learned the tricks of make-up.

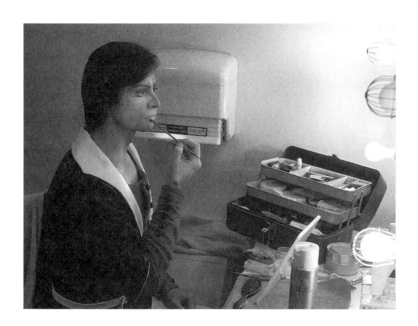

I enjoyed touring in the beginning, but after a while, it became a bore. I'd put myself on automatic pilot. Little tricks helped, like learning what to pack and what not to pack. I quickly learned not to go straight to the hotel check-in with a busload of sixty other dancers, but to go and sit in the restaurant, get a bite to eat, and then check in – that, or try to be the first one off the bus. There were dancers who guarded that front seat on the bus with their lives. You could always find Laszlo Surmeyan and his wife, Lorna Geddes, at the front of the bus, with Lorna knitting away like Mme. Defarge. She wasn't the only one. Many of the women – and some of the men, too – would knit, do needlepoint, or hook rugs. I spent a lot of time reading newspapers, which helped pass the time. I was never better informed than I was when touring.

In the dos and don'ts of touring, missing the bus – or rather delaying the bus – was seen as a major crime. I will never, ever, forget the day my alarm failed to ring. I was called by the touring manager. In less than five minutes, without a shower, I was out of my room, checked out, and on that damned bus. As I walked to the back, I had to pass rows of tired, irritated, angry dancers. Everyone else was there, ready and glaring at me. Still, I was lucky to make it in time. Sometimes, the bus would leave without dancers, and they would have to make their own way to the next venue.

That bus was a giant apartment, populated by forty very different individuals. We had to learn to get along. It was through touring that I learned to read people's moods. I had to, if I wanted to keep my friends. My whole world was the company. We were almost con-stantly together – in the bus, in the theatre, on a plane, or more often sitting around waiting for any or all of these. We really got to know each other, warts and all, all the little foibles, magnified by too much constant contact. It produced a different kind of respect for people, a different sensitivity, because we had to live and work together.

There was no star system in touring, no special treatment for anyone. Except, that is, for Rudolf. When Rudolf toured with us, he emphatically did not use the bus, but went ahead in a chauffeured luxury car. This car was a wonder of the world, a lime-green Cadillac with white seats inside and white vinyl on the roof. It was the ugliest thing I had ever seen. "Looks like brothel," was how Rudolf would proudly point it out. He always travelled at night, immediately after the performance, jumping into the car and moving on to the next city. He often tried to get me to ride with him, an offer I brightly refused. The rest of us usually followed on, in the bus, the next day. Most dancers preferred to do this, but in many ways, what Rudolf did made sense. You were wired after the performance and couldn't sleep, so why not travel?

Each place has its own particular memory. Paris was expensive hotels, where we all checked out of the hotel in which we were booked, because we thought eleven dollars a night was too expensive. Antigonish, Nova Scotia, was the snow blizzard, which was so bad the bus had to pull off the road, and we stayed in a hotel without power, several of us in one room, huddled together for warmth. Montreal was food poisoning from fast food.

Of all the places we went, New York was the most exciting – perhaps because at that time it was the dance capital of the world. Through most of the 1970s, summers meant a hot and humid season in New York. I can still feel the heat of those sweltering New York summers and I still remember the cockroaches. Most memorably, I was walking back to the hotel along Central Park West late one night, when, on a grate outside, I could see something shimmering in the dark. From a distance, I couldn't quite see what it was. As I got closer, I realized in horror that the grate was swarming with roaches, like something from a Cronenberg movie. I walked around them, hoping – faint hope – that they would not find their way into the hotel.

Our second season in the city was marked by the blackout of '75, when there was a power failure across the city. The company was performing *Coppélia* when the lights at the Met went out. The audience filed out in orderly fashion, and everyone went home. I wasn't at the theatre at the time. I had done a matinee that afternoon, and had eaten and gone back to the hotel. I looked out of my window to find that everyone had their high beams on and all the cars were honking their horns, while a lady in a nightdress stood in the middle of an intersection, resolutely directing the traffic. I went downstairs and, by candlelight, helped escort the women from the company back to their rooms.

That was New York to me, always something different. Like the night when I swore I saw a UFO. No, I was not crazy or drugged, there were five or six of us, and we all saw it – dancers Karyn Tessmer, Cynthia Lucas, Vanessa Harwood, Tomas Schramek, and David Roxander were all right there with me. We were walking back towards our hotel when it appeared: there, in the sky, a disc of light that got larger and larger as it descended to – where else would it go – right above the Met. It looked like the starship out of *Close Encounters of a Third Kind*. We headed towards the Met, ready for adventure, but when we were still quite a distance away, it collapsed into itself and was gone.

New York also meant party time, particularly when Rudolf was with us. He was constantly invited to dinners, receptions, and parties, and he thought nothing of asking groups of us to come along with him. I guess we became his entourage – what's a star without one? I don't know what those footing the bill thought, but we loved it. Number one, it was a free meal, which, given our princely salaries, was always appreciated. It was also an interesting experience to see how the rich and famous lived. We had just given a performance; now we got to watch the performance after the performance. We'd sit observing and listening to unreal (to us) discussions of where the best bargain for a yacht was. A steal at $1.5 million U.S.

These were also good times just to sit and listen to Rudolf talk —
about ballets, about art, and about movies. He was a great movie fan.
Rudolf was insatiably curious; he was interested in anything and
everything, except perhaps politics. I don't think I ever heard him
discuss politics, which did not mean that he was unaware. About
everything else, he obviously knew so much. Watching Rudolf surrounded by his wealthy and influential friends, I realized that he
enjoyed playing with the rich and famous. He seemed very comfortable and secure surrounded by these people, almost as if they were
offering him a form of protection. It was as if he were afraid that one
day the KGB would come up to him on the street, or in a restaurant, or
in a hotel, or in his home, and kill him. This was a very real fear of
his. On top of the mountain, surrounded by the rich, he could at least
feel secure that, if anything happened to him, these were people who
would try to do something about it.

New York was the place where we felt our reputations were vali-
dated. Canadian dancers are as prone as other Canadian artists to feel
they are only really successful when Americans tell them they are. In
New York, through all our seasons there, the critics gave us their blessing. It was nice to have this accolade. It was also nice to be recognized
when you walked out of the theatre, although at first I wasn't entirely
comfortable with it. That first year in New York, I once walked out of
the stage door to have someone ask me if Mr. Augustyn was still in the
dressing room. "He's still back in there," I replied, and went on my way
out into the night. Later, I got to like the attention and was happy to
sign autographs.

Life at the National Ballet in the 1970s was not just the classics.
Although the Prince mould fitted me well, it never seemed to be
enough. I was always looking for ways to break out of it, and it turned

out that there were several opportunities to do this. The first, Ballet Revue, was a small summer touring troupe that a few of us set up for ourselves. It gave us the opportunity to experiment, and we had tremendous success with it.

The idea came from Ann Ditchburn, who was then in the corps and was an aspiring choreographer. Ann was a great friend of Karen's; they talked, and started pulling together a troupe that in the end consisted of both of them, me, Tomas Schramek, Cynthia Lucas, David Roxander, and Karyn Tessmer. Our aim was to show that the dancers from the National Ballet were not classical automatons, that we could also be creative, cutting-edge dancers. We were sure we could be just as hip as the folks at Toronto Dance Theatre. At least, we would try.

From beginning to end, it was chaotic. At any one point, most of us did not know what was going on. Perhaps this was because we were foolish enough to try to devise a program democratically. There was no artistic director — everyone had their say. Ann was to create a beginning and end, with the rest of the program to be decided collectively, and we had a scant two and a half weeks to put the whole thing together. It was all done on a shoestring budget. The National was helpful with props and costumes, but they charged us for them. Nothing was free. It was a financial risk, because six of us were directors of the company, and we were responsible for any financial losses.

Peter Sever, who had been assistant to the National Ballet's general manager, and was now out on his own as an agent, solicited a donation from Imperial Oil, and got us bookings across the country. Mostly, we were to play small theatres, but we were also booked into the National Arts Centre Opera House in Ottawa and the Queen Elizabeth Theatre in Vancouver. To our astonishment, the performances sold out. The show was promoted on the names of Kain and Augustyn, but also as being something that was definitely not the National Ballet. True, we were National Ballet people, but we were renegades, or so the line went. We were young and effervescent. We had created something new for the world to see. That was all announced to the world before we had any very clear of idea of what it was this "something new" was. We had to come up with it. And fast.

Ann was a creative force, but she had problems communicating. From the beginning, she was very comfortable with the women, and could deal with and work with them well. But she had a battle with the men. She was very nervous and hyper, and in the studio, I felt that she believed I was trying to dominate or attack her. Yet all I really wanted was for her to give me the choreography and the ideas behind it. I think her original intention was to do something underground, which wouldn't have involved critics or large audiences. All of a sudden, the project had grown into something far larger than she had originally intended. She had a lot to contend with. She was responsible for the choreography – but the decision-making was collective. Nervous herself, she also had a bunch of very nervous dancers to deal with. We would find her off in the park, drinking cognac with Karyn Tessmer, and trying to talk Karyn back into the studio. Karyn had been hired to help fill classical roles. She had only just started work as a professional dancer, and when she was asked to do "Sleeping Beauty," she became very anxious. Who could blame her for being scared? I was.

We had a very loose schedule – everyone would do their own warm-up, and we'd get together at about noon. We rehearsed at Toronto Workshop Theatre on George Street, which we got cheaply. In rehearsals, there was always the odd amount of hash and marijuana around. Looking back, I don't know how we did what we did, but somehow we pieced it together.

Ann choreographed and performed an opening and closing number, and a piece from her ballet, *Nelligan*. Tomas did another piece from *Nelligan*. Karen and David did a funny "tall lady–short guy" piece, a skit based on a ballet competition, which I announced. I did a personal essay, a dance piece using my spoken voice describing the movement. This had its origins in a radio program I had done, "Personal Essay," for the CBC. We threw in a few standard crowd pleasers, like *Corsair* and *Sleeping Beauty*, demonstrating that we were maybe not quite as cutting edge as we liked to think.

We had to drop some things. Ann wanted to have us presenting things on stage vocally. She gathered us in a group-therapy session, and secretly taped everyone spilling the beans on their thoughts about their lives and insecurities. She wanted to use the edited tape as music. When we heard what she had done, one thing everyone agreed should go was someone talking about masturbating with a refrigerator. Even for our newfound rebel selves that was going a little too far.

We were due to open at the Shaw Festival, at Niagara-on-the-Lake. The night before that first Shaw performance, in a blind panic, I spent the whole night in the car in the hotel parking lot. It wasn't just that I was nervous; I was absolutely terrified. Nothing was going right. We had disorganized rehearsals. Ann, who had started it all off, was back in the park again drinking cognac with Karyn Tessmer, doing her best to give Karyn emotional support. Karen Kain was still nervous about it all, feeling she had had insufficient rehearsal time. She always aimed to be perfect. What happened to perfection? she would ask. Give me a break, I thought. Perfection? We'll be lucky if we can make it through the night. It seemed like everything was a mess, and nothing was going to get done right. Then there was Peter Sever, who must also have been terrified. "Where's the show?" he kept asking. "Where's the show? You have twenty-one bookings across Canada."

On opening night, we all made it to the theatre, which in itself was something of a miracle. But the real miracle was that, from the first bars of music, we knew we had a show. Somehow, don't ask me how, we just geared up our professionalism and locked everything down on the stage. We were there to do something different, and, damn it, we all did. The audience gave an overwhelming response,

Above: The Ballet Revue gang. From left: Tomas Schramek, Cynthia Lucas,
David Roxander, Karen Kain, me, and Ann Ditchburn.
Below: With Karen, in Afternoon of a Faun.

and the reviews were excellent. We went on from there. It gave us the strength. Once we got opening night over with, that gave us energy. All of a sudden we had that magical thing, confidence.

Ballet Revue was a highlight for all of us. It even managed to make us a little money. We hired a film company to make a two-camera record of it all, which survives on tape, unedited. You can barely make anything out, so we have nothing left of the experiences but our memories, and a few photographs. When we returned to the National after the tour, we felt like the cat's meow. It had been great. But then, we had always known it would be, hadn't we? We were very proud of ourselves, and not a little cocky with it.

We had a meeting with Alexander Grant and said we wanted to do this again. His response was firm, and not at all what we had expected. Alexander said either you become part of the company as Ballet Revue, and do it under the company auspices, or take a leave of absence and do it on your own. If he had played it right, he could have had it both ways: let us do it, and keep the National's name closely associated with it – but that wasn't the way he put it. We wanted to maintain our little group independently. He didn't want that, and there was a huge break right then and there. We had a vote on it and, out of the group, Karen and Tomas wanted to stay within the company, while Cindy and David were unsure. Only Ann and I wanted to take a leave. This lack of unity ended our little venture into rebellion and entrepreneurship.

Throughout the 1970s, the National ran a choreographic workshop that highlighted the works of young choreographers. Within the company at that time, there were three aspiring dancemakers: James Kudelka, who has gone on to become artistic director of the company; Ann Ditchburn, our Ballet Revue mastermind; and Constantin Patsalas. The workshops provided another opportunity to dance outside the traditional classical mode, an opportunity we all relished.

The highlight for me was Kudelka's *Washington Square*, which brought James to the fore as a choreographer and introduced the National to a blazing talent in its midst that had so far gone unrecognized. I don't think Cynthia Lucas had had a single acting lesson in her life. Acting just came naturally to her, and her performance as Catherine in *Washington Square* was unsurpassed. I loved doing *Washington Square* with her, she was so convincing in the role. But then, she was always someone else on the stage, she was never Cindy Lucas. Cindy gave you a sense that, between the dressing room and the stage, a transformation occurred. She was an actor, a true actor.

James choreographed *Washington Square* on Cindy and me, although we didn't open it when it was mounted for the full company. One of the great talents James has is that he casts extremely well. He is very good at reading people's strengths. Consequently, he used Cindy a lot, because she danced well, was enthusiastic, they got along, and most importantly, she could act. Her transformation into a dance actress was something quite special for all of us to see.

Washington Square was one of the few opportunities for me to play an out-and-out cad. The choreography was fluid, and you could bring more acting ability to it than you could with the stylized movement of the classics. I liked working with James in the studio, because he was so focussed. He saw clearly what any dancer could do for him, and was always very exact and so good at explaining the approach to movement. You never felt that you did something that displeased him. He either liked what he saw, or, if he didn't, he would never let you know, but would work with it, and make out of it something that he did like.

Cindy and I had both made a point of reading the book by Henry James, so that, when we started work, we were both on top of the story and our characters. For us, it was an adventure. It was the first time I experienced how easy it was to learn and create a role when you are truly immersed in it, when you become that person. The fear, tension, and nerves are gone, you really are with the character, and there is nothing extraneous that can interfere. It was a revelation to me, a fabulous tool. There is a moment in Catherine's living room when my character surveys the room, not just to look at how beautiful the artwork is, but also to assess its monetary value. Trying to get that across was a challenge; it had to be very subtle. There were other workshop productions, but *Washington Square* was for me the most memorable.

The opportunity to dance different and challenging pieces came more rarely within the confines of the main company. *Monument for a Dead Boy*, first choreographed by Rudi van Dantzig in 1965, was one of the standouts here. The National acquired the ballet from the Dutch some ten years after its original production. Rudi van Dantzig now feels that the ballet is dated, but I think it is still timely. In its day, dealing openly with the subject of homosexuality on the ballet stage, as this ballet did, was seen as highly controversial. It was exciting to be working with Rudi van Dantzig on an extremely powerful piece. So much of the story hinged on my abilities not only as a dancer, but also as an interpreter. *Monument for a Dead Boy* was a mesmerizing piece, the story of an alienated man at odds with the world around him. His parents are enormously powerful figures in the ballet, almost like monsters on the stage, grotesque in both behaviour and movement. The ballet focusses on the boy's attempts to find love, first with a woman, later with a man, and his subsequent sense of guilt.

Rudi van Dantzig came to cast the ballet, and then much later to put the final touches to it five or six days before the first performance. He was very nervous and high-strung, always seeming to be in a great rush. His intensity is what I remember most about him. He would get on my nerves with his "Yes, go-go-go-go-go-go-go, yesh-Frank-yesh." The music is going, and you are working like mad, and there is somebody going *go-go-go-go-go*. I felt like saying go *away*, you're bothering me. It was almost as if he wanted to do it himself. Regardless of how much you were giving, still he wanted more. If nothing else, we knew from his choreography that he needed a sense of urgency and tension. Rudi liked the body movements over-exaggerated, particularly on the upper body, which was a different approach to classical ballet, where you are quite rigid on top. He also liked a great amount of travelling across the stage in a millisecond of time, with very quick, sharp movements. It was a unique style of movement, something new to work my body around.

Monument was important for me in two ways. It was the first time I experienced a contemporary ballet in which the man was the focus of the story. I could be recognized here as an artist in my own right, not as part of a partnership. That was important to me. On a more personal level, the story had another resonance. The parents in the ballet constantly fought.

Four Schumann Pieces, another contemporary piece acquired by the company in 1976, was more abstract. The second of three Dutch works acquired around this time, it had a minimal storyline, sketching the passage of a man through his life. The beauty was in the way the choreographer Hans van Manen used Schumann's music. In some ways, I considered van Manen a minimalist, because he didn't over-choreograph. He would never cram in too many steps for no particular reason. Van Manen's choreography comes directly to the point, with no wastage of time or movement.

Four Schumann Pieces was a huge technical challenge, partly because it had been choreographed on one of the great dancers of our generation, the Royal Ballet's Anthony Dowell. Anthony was a lefty, and although van Manen kindly said I could do the more difficult chaîné turns to the right, there were still a lot of left turns in the ballet. Anthony was good at turns and had exquisite balance. He also had a long body, and the choreography was designed to show the lines of the body beautifully. There are a few double tours, but no great leaps.

In short, this wasn't power dancing; it was far more intricate. The steps were woven, rather than stamped. All very Anthony, except for the arms, which were very Hans, bent at the elbow, palms raised forward and slightly turned out.

As the principal dancer in a ballet that was technically so extremely difficult, I felt more exposed than usual. I always felt exposed on stage, as though I were opening my soul to the audience, and I was always afraid of this exposure. At the beginning of the ballet, I'd stand on stage, do my warm-up and, at first, feel relaxed and excited. Then there always seemed to be a fifteen-minute wait while the audience was filtering in. Fears would start to rush through my mind, and I would stifle them, telling myself there was really nothing to fear – I was well-rehearsed, I was prepared. Then the stage manager would call everyone to their places. The house lights would go down, the audience fall silent, and I would stand there thinking, I don't want to be here. I want to take a cab and go home. That thought would be interrupted by the whirr of the curtains going up. I'd look out at the black cave of the audience, and only at that moment would the inspiration come back.

This gamut of emotions, one that I ran through with most performances, always seemed more extreme with this piece, because there was nothing in it to hide behind – no story, and no great technical tricks. It was a thoughtful piece of pure dancing, with only a hint of story, not the kind of ballet to bring the house down. There is, however, a section in the last movement that is extremely fast, and if done well, it can look outstanding. *Four Schumann Pieces* was a challenge, as any ballet would be when made to measure on someone else. Fortunately, van Manen was easy with changes, as he wanted the ballet to look good on whoever did it.

Out of this came an experimental CBC Radio interview, "Personal Essay," which was suggested to me by Douglas Byers. I chose a piece of music, the first solo of *Four Schumann Pieces*. Then Douglas asked me

Above: In Four Schumann Pieces, *the signature van Manen arms.*
Below: With Tomas Schramek in Maurice Béjart's Songs of a Wayfarer.

to describe first what I needed to do to make my body work to accomplish the steps. We ran the music again, and this time I went through it, describing what I needed to think about in order to make the steps work with the right feeling. The two tracks were then placed in the music, as a sound collage. It was a huge success, and it was aired across Canada seventy-five times. Interestingly, after it had aired I received a lot of fan mail from blind people.

In 1977, Karen and I were taught the choreography of Jerome Robbins's *Afternoon of a Faun*, a neo-classical pas de deux showing two dancers in a studio setting. Robbins came for a very short visit to vet what we were doing. We had expected a rather mean individual, since he had that reputation, but he turned out to be perfectly pleasant to work with, in the short afternoon we spent with him. He refined what we learned from the restager, and gave his approval. *Faun* is harder than it looks. In it, two individuals, working together, look past each other, as if in a mirror, which becomes an additional partner. It's a brilliant, simple work, evoking a hot summer day. I liked the ballet, but I hated my costume. Black tights, white socks. I hated black tights, because I thought my legs were so skinny, and they made them look even skinnier. It might have looked good on someone with the thighs and legs of a line-backer, but not on me.

Alexander Grant was always looking for works that would sit well with his dancers. He particularly wanted to bring in Belgian choreographer Maurice Béjart's *Songs of a Wayfarer* for me and Tomas Schramek. He called Béjart and asked if he could have the work.

"Have you got two good boys?" Béjart asked.

"Oh yes," Alexander said, "I've got two very good boys."

"I'll have to teach it to them," Béjart said.

"When can you come?" Alexander asked.

"Oh, I can't come, you'll have to send them to me," said Béjart. So, in the summer of 1979, after a season in London, Alexander sent

Tomas and me off to Brussels to learn the choreography of *Songs of a Wayfarer*, set to Mahler's *Leider eines fahrenden Gesellen*. Alexander's acquisition of this work for the National Ballet was something of a coup, as Béjart did not give out his works to everyone who asked. A pas de deux for two men, it was originally choreographed for Erik Bruhn and Rudolf Nureyev, and was reputed to have been about their personal relationship. Bruhn dropped out in the early stages, and Paolo Bertoluzzi, Béjart's leading dancer, took over his role, dancing the ballet with Rudolf.

When Tomas and I arrived in Brussels, Béjart was at first nowhere to be seen. We spent five or six days in Brussels, learning the choreography from one of his coaches. Finally, near the end of our time there, Béjart came into the studio to see how we were doing. He was happy with our technique and encouraging about our interpretations. Later, he told us that we were among the best he had ever seen in the piece. The few corrections he gave all had to do with feeling rather than technique. At the end of the session, we were invited back to his apartment. Off the living room, he showed us a large, intricately carved wooden door, which he opened to reveal a smaller room with a carpet and cushions scattered about. He was a Buddhist, and this was his room for devotions. We felt honoured to be invited in, and it was there that we sat, talking.

I asked him what *Songs of a Wayfarer* meant to him. He turned the question back at me and asked me what it meant to me. I told him that for me the ballet was really the story of one man, his younger self, open and innocent, and his older self, weighed down by his sense of responsibility and reality. It was the child in the man dying, a coming to maturity. Then Béjart turned to Tomas and asked what it meant to him. Tomas explained his take on the pas de deux, which was similar to mine. I then tried again, and asked Béjart a second time what it meant to him, but he would have none of it. "I can't tell you that," he said, "it's far too personal."

By 1979, my partnership with Karen had moved onto shaky ground. When we worked together in the early days, we knew intuitively what the other person felt. Then, around this time, Karen began to demand things from me in a way she had never done before. It happened quite suddenly, after one of her trips to France, which she frequently made in those days to work with Roland Petit. It was almost as though she had picked up an entirely new way of working. She was more anxious, had more of a sense of urgency, a "let's get on with it" attitude.

The mood of the previous season had been excellent, and I had been glad to get back into the studio after the break. I felt physically well, and that I was developing, but suddenly something was wrong, something had happened. I had the feeling that Karen thought she was developing faster than me, that she was more important than me, and that she didn't need me any more. "I need you to be more like this, look at me here," she would say. I was *always* aware of where to look. She was almost never out of my sight, and if she was out of my sight, I was always aware of what she was doing. "Look at me, look at me like you love me, look at me with some fire," she would say. All of a sudden, she was imposing on me her idea of what she needed from me. I felt my ideas did not matter. It was like someone had put a rock in my stomach. I thought, every other couple in dance behaves like this, but not us. I thought we were on another level here, that we were so in tune that these things did not have to be spoken. I never criticized Karen's ability, or demanded what I needed from her emotionally, because I knew that, on that stage, when it counted, it would always be there. I hoped and thought that, after all these years, I was doing the same for her. It disturbed me that she no longer felt that way.

Our personal relationship had always been full of ups and downs. It lasted for a total of seven years, but during those seven years, she left me twice. We had got back together after both those episodes, but when she came to visit me while I was working with Béjart in Brussels, we both decided to put an end to the relationship, because it was not what either of us wanted or needed. We did not make any decision to stop dancing together, but agreed to go our separate personal ways. It was a very hard time. She cried. I didn't; I was beyond crying. It was a painful, but inevitable, thing. It was clear to me that I was trying to hold on to something that was no longer there. For a while, I held a faint hope that she would be back, because I loved her deeply. There was a lot of hurt.

I don't think we were totally compatible as lovers. We were to a degree, and there was certainly a great trust and understanding. We knew how to laugh and cry together; we were so comfortable doing things together. But Karen's temperament and my temperament on a day-to-day basis, her attack and drive compared to my more laid-back approach, never really worked. I felt she didn't have some of the things I needed, and I don't think that she got everything she needed from a man in me, emotionally – I would sometimes become very distant and feel I needed to get away, I needed some privacy. When you are working with someone and seeing them privately, you need some time on your own. That's why we never lived together, although we each owned our own homes, and that says a lot, right there. On tour, we'd share a room. We'd work together, dine together, sleep together. We had the same friends. Everything was one world. That may have been too much, too saturating. Nothing new came in from outside. Maybe that's why, in the end, we both married someone from outside the world of ballet.

The evening after we had decided on our break-up, I had one of the strangest experiences of my life. I was staying at the Hotel Metropole, in Brussels, an old hotel with creaky floors, where you could hear people in the hallway. I had gone to bed and was about ready to fall asleep, when I heard someone walking down the hallway. My door didn't open, but suddenly there was a *click* on the ceramic tiles inside the door and then the sound of steps on the floor in my room. First, the steps went to the left side of my bed, then around to the right. Neon lights shone into the room from the outside and, when I looked, I saw there was no one there. Then creak, creak, creak again, to the foot of the bed. I was alert and uneasy. I sat up in bed. "Look," I said, "I'm really tired. Please go away." I then lay back down and listened as the footsteps went out, onto the tile, and out of my room and down the hallway. I believe in spirits, and I may be more receptive to them than I might like or want. One thing I know: there was someone or something in my room that night, but I didn't care. I didn't want any messages. All I wanted was to sleep, I was so tired and drained, as well as being very, very frightened.

I didn't realize it at the time, but the end of the relationship would be a turning point in our partnership. I cherished the relationship, and I cherished the partnership, and, if you asked me which one I cherished more, I don't know that I could have an answer to that, because they were so intertwined. The partnership lasted after the relationship was over, but not with any great intensity. There was a need now, on both our parts, to be independent of each other.

CHAPTER
———————————
10

Berlin Interlude

By 1980, I was becoming increasingly tired of dancing some of the roles that I had been dancing on a regular basis for eight years. High on the list of problem parts for me was the Prince in *Swan Lake. Elite Syncopations*, a modern work by Kenneth MacMillan, was another ballet I wanted to give a rest. I did that ad nauseam. Basically, my role in that ballet was to play a forklift truck. All I ever did in that ballet was lift. I did it over and over and over again, and I was beginning to feel I was just a machine. With both of these roles, I felt I had nothing left to offer. I went to see Alexander Grant to ask if I could take a year off from both ballets. This was not something that Alexander wanted to hear. He suspected that I wanted out because I found lifting Karen — who at around a hundred-plus pounds weighed more than most ballerinas — hard on my back. That absolutely was not the case.

———————————

As the butler, in the Berlin Opera production of Miss Julie.

My wanting out of the ballets proved to be another turning point with Karen. Like Alexander, she didn't appreciate it. After all, I was asking to not do some of the most popular works that we did together. I understand everything about professionalism, about being consistent and being there when needed. That was what I was trained to do. But I was also trained as an artist, and I wasn't able to give much more, particularly to *Swan Lake*. What I wanted was a break. I didn't want to give up the ballets forever. I stressed that I was willing to do anything and everything else, but Alexander Grant saw it as a slap in the face. He said I should just do it; it was important for the company. He was looking at it from the point of view of the box office, and a "show must go on" mentality. In Alexander's eyes, I was not behaving like a trouper.

All the arguments in the book were thrown at me: do it while you can, think of how many years you have left to dance, the audience wants you, Karen needs you. There was a lot of pressure, including pressure from Karen. In the end, I think Karen understood, although I don't think she ever quite forgave me. In the face of all this opposition, it was more important for me to follow my instincts than to follow the company's line. I was arrogant enough to believe that the position I had in the company would allow me to refuse roles. I didn't think I was being temperamental, although that is how others saw it. What I was trying to do was keep my best for the company, and that was something they didn't seem to understand. Reluctantly, I agreed to do one *Swan Lake* with Karen, and the company arranged to bring in guest partners for her for the rest, as there was really no one else within the company at that time who could partner her in it. She was too tall for the other principals.

Even with this accommodation, I was still restless. I felt my performances were suffering. To me, dancing was a form of physical conversation, one I held with other dancers and the audience. I wanted, through movement, to move the emotions. It didn't really matter to me whether the audience wanted to laugh or cry or yell — as long as they were moved, I felt my job was done. Of course, I was always happier when they felt the way I wanted them to feel – that was the greatest satisfaction of all. For a long time, I had tried to dance in a way that would please other people, would make *them* happy. But finally I had realized that this didn't work; I had to work from within, to listen to my own voice and be honest with myself. Only when I was doing this, dancing from the heart, was I truly happy with what I had done. Lately, I had been feeling that I was able to do this less than I should. It was time for a change. The regularity of the company's seasons, too, was becoming monotonous: the O'Keefe in Toronto, summers at the Metropolitan, either a tour in eastern Canada or western Canada. Both the venues and repertoire were predictable. I wanted to explore new ideas and new movement. I had had enough of fairy tales. I needed to do more contemporary classical pieces and to get out of the mould of the prince. Rudi van Dantzig's *Monument for a Dead Boy* had been a challenge I enjoyed. Hans van Manen's *Four Schumann Pieces* had been equally interesting. But there were so few new works, only ever one or two a year. I wanted more.

I decided to try dancing in Europe. Maurice Béjart had offered me a contract to dance in Brussels, but the pay was poor, and Béjart would not allow anyone to guest elsewhere. He also would not guarantee roles. My National Ballet School friend Michael McKim was dancing with the company at the time, and he told me a little of what it was like to work there. It was a madhouse, he said. Béjart worked on whims. If he liked you, that was great. If not, well, that could be a problem. Despite this, I was tempted. Béjart's work was so unique and innovative, and he had some of the best male dancers in the world in his company at that time – Paolo Bortoluzzi and Jorge Donn were both there. I thought about it for a while, but in the end decided that dancing only Béjart's work might be too confining. Brussels felt like too much of a risk. So my agent, Alex Dubé, set about finding a

company that needed a male principal. The Opera House in West
Berlin came back with the most interesting offer.

I asked Alexander for a year-long leave of absence to dance in
Berlin. Again, Alexander was not happy. "Who's going to see you
in Berlin?" he asked. He felt I was abandoning ship for something he
did not see as worthwhile. I made it clear that I did not want to leave
permanently, I only wanted to learn new works and dance with different people for a while. I felt I needed to do this if I were to improve
artistically, but I wanted the National to remain my home. Berlin was
interesting because it had works I really wanted to dance: Balanchine's
Apollo, more van Manen pieces, Nureyev's *Nutcracker*. It had dancers I
wanted to work with: Eva Evdokimova, Galina Panova, and Valery
Panov. None of this was understood at the National. I think what
concerned Alexander most was how he would approach the board
about it. He believed he was giving me everything I needed – and if he
was doing that, why on earth did I want to leave? He had brought in
ballets like *Songs of a Wayfarer* specifically for me. Yet still I wanted to
go. In the end, we found a compromise. I would sign on with Berlin
for a year, while agreeing to do a number of performances for the
National. I committed myself to a year of commuting between Berlin
and Toronto, without having any idea of how hard that could be.

For a whole year through the 1980–81 season, I lived in a kind of
no-man's-land, making the Berlin-Toronto round trip maybe twelve
times, and never really living in either city. I did not come to know
many people in Berlin, and, although I missed the company and my
friends in Toronto, I had decided at that point that friends and emotional attachments were not important. All my efforts were going into
developing a career that I really believed would soon be over. I was
twenty-seven, and I could see my older colleagues slowing down. Even
at my age, I was enduring more pain, and it took me longer to recover
than it had when I was seventeen. I felt I had only a few years left, and
that I had to make the best of them. Then I looked at Nureyev. He

was doing 260 performances a year. I was doing eighty. I knew I was capable of doing much more than that. To make the best of what I had before it was too late, I was happy to double my workload, expand my repertoire, and live out of a suitcase for a year.

At first sight, I found Berlin depressing. You could feel the enclosure of the city, which was still isolated behind the Iron Curtain. There wasn't the freedom of New York, or the vivaciousness of Paris, or the distinctive personality of London. The atmosphere was colder, and I think that had a lot to do with the utilitarian architecture. Berlin wasn't a welcoming city, but that didn't matter to me. I was there to be stimulated by my new company. I took an apartment on Bismarckstrasse, a few blocks from the Opera House, and was soon hard at work.

The Berlin Opera House was unlike anything else I had seen. Some two thousand people were working there, and everything was under one roof — costume-makers, set-builders, the orchestra, eighty or ninety dancers. The stage was fabulous, deep, wide, and flat, like the Met, where they have another stage behind the stage. The seating arrangement within the house was such that everyone, wherever he or she sat, had a good view. The acoustics were excellent, and the backstage technology was phenomenal — hydraulic lifts, trapdoors, the works. The company was international, with dancers from all over the world. English was the operating language, with class taught in French. That was a disappointment. I had hoped to pick up another language as a side benefit of the stay. After the first class with the company, I thought I would try out my German. It was a hot day, and I went over to a group of women at the barre and introduced myself. *"Bis du heiss?"* I asked, thinking I had asked if they were hot. They looked at me, and, one by one, walked away. I wondered what was wrong until someone later told me that I had asked if they were horny.

My first real friend in Berlin was the artistic director of the ballet, Gert Reinholm. Gert was a striking man with piercing blue eyes, a good artistic director who was very well connected and had an innate political sense. Gert knew the ins and outs of the Berlin Opera House. He also loved ballet and enjoyed the process of programming works and casting dancers. In a series of many long conversations, I learned from Gert how a European opera/ballet house worked, everything from the operational structure to budgeting, to the treatment of dancers, to programming, sets, and costume design. It was an intriguing introduction to the world of the artistic director.

Gert was half a dictator, and half a free spirit. If there were any dispute within the company, or with the union, he would take a very hard line. On the other hand, one-to-one with dancers, he was flexible and would try to understand and be accommodating. I became a confidant because I was part of the regime, yet at the same time, as a principal guest artist, I wasn't. Gert used me as a sounding board, and I was flattered that he would ask for my views, although I couldn't provide much help other than listening. I felt free enough to give my opinion, which was always well taken. Through Gert, I learned a lot about ballet as a business. In the short year I was in Berlin, I had a better view of how the company was run than I ever did of the National, because I had a direct line to the director.

Frau Gudrun Leben was my main coach in Berlin. I quickly developed a love-hate relationship with Gudrun. She was a short little thing with a bulldog mentality, quite old to my young eyes, with straight, short hair dyed strawberry-blond. She was the sort of person whose look would accuse you, just because you were standing there. She taught in English with a heavy German accent, demonstrating the steps, and then you'd have to prove to her that you could actually do them. She had an "I don't care who you are, you have to show me" attitude. Everyone was absolutely terrified of her, and with good cause.

The first new ballet I did in Berlin was Hans van Manen's *Five Tangos*. I had learned the choreography privately with Gudrun, and I thought I knew it. Then we did a run-through with everyone. When

With Diane Bell, in Five Tangos,
one of the modern works I added to my rep in Berlin.

the music started, I missed my first entrance. She stopped the tape. "Frank, you have to at least get the first step right," she said. I was a principal guest artist, and right off the bat she was treating me like a green first-year corps member. "You're right," I said. "The first step, and the last step." She laughed, I laughed, and the company then started laughing. From that moment on, I think maybe because I stood up to her and didn't allow that embarrassing moment to shake me, we got along extremely well. She had a very difficult life through the war, in Berlin. Her entire family was wiped out. She developed that tough and aggressive personality because of the life she had led, but she still knew how to laugh. Despite all she went through, she never lost that. Gudrun could respect you, but it was very clear that you had to earn it. Some people didn't like being bullied, and she did tend to bully, but I grew to really like her. It was clear to me that she got good results.

Five Tangos was a contemporary piece, full of Hans van Manen's signature moves. He likes the arms lifted, angled almost at a right angle, and turned outward. The work is full of switches — turned in, turned out, quick runs and jumps, changes of direction. It is interesting, intricate choreography, but since I had already worked with van Manen, I knew his style. My solo was fabulous, musically intricate, and had tremendous impact if done well and fast. I thanked Daniel Seillier for training me how to move quickly, because I needed every bit of speed I could muster to get through it.

I had gone to Berlin with the goal of learning new works, and I wasn't disappointed. One of my favourite ballets from the Berlin rep was *Twilight*. Another Hans van Manen piece, it is an extended pas de deux depicting a relationship that is more violent than tender. Hans van Manen couldn't make it to Berlin to teach it, so I went to Amsterdam with principal dancer Charlotte Butler to learn the choreography. We worked first with a restager, then Hans van Manen saw it and put his blessing on it. It was really an exhausting ballet. It's only about twelve minutes long, but it was very difficult — partly because it goes non-stop, and partly because the van Manen style was then relatively new to me. It also had an unusual setting – the backdrop is a factory, and the couple are working class. It was the first time in my dance career that I saw anything remotely like Hamilton on the stage, and it was about as far from the classics as you could get. If I had wanted to expand my range, this was definitely a step in the right direction.

Gert saw the final rehearsal, and he kept saying, You are not standing right. The Dutch dancer Hans Ebbelaar, who had performed the role in Berlin, had an ape-like stance, but all those years of classical training meant that it wasn't possible for me to stand like an ape. I was sorry to disappoint Gert, but I had to do it in a different way, yet still get the right feeling. The man isn't too intelligent, he has few manners, and it would be in character for him to burp at the dinner table and fart after sex. That was the feeling I was looking for.

One of the great neo-classical works for the male dancer is Balanchine's *Apollo*, set to music by Stravinsky, and I was looking forward to dancing it in Berlin. Prior to this I had danced in three other Balanchine ballets, *Serenade* (where the man does little more than walk on and lift), *Four Temperaments*, and *Concerto Barocco*. Balanchine is not my favourite choreographer, but I loved *Apollo*. I foolishly thought I understood the piece, but then I started rehearsing, and I quickly realized that I didn't understand it at all. The steps I knew, but I absolutely did not understand the movement, so the first few days working on the ballet were a struggle. On top of this, there was the challenge of Stravinsky, whose music is difficult for most dancers, it is so intricate. You have to count – and really, really know the music. Only if you completely memorize it can you stop counting. The more I worked it, the more exact I became, and the more relaxed I was.

I was so eager to do justice to what I thought was a work of genius. I was definitely intimidated by the piece and by an image I carried in my mind of Peter Martins, the great Balanchine dancer, who was blessed with the looks of Apollo, in the role. To me, Martins really was Apollo – an aloof and arrogant god. I danced this ballet with Eva Evdokimova, Galina Panova, and Diane Bell, and, although in the end I did it quite well, I was never a natural Apollo. I think I was close, but I was too human. I had flaws. Being a god didn't come naturally to me.

Apollo was difficult enough, but even more of a challenge was *Miss Julie*. An adaptation of a Strindberg play, *Miss Julie* was choreographed by Birgit Cullberg in 1950. I played the butler, a role I never felt I was able to master. I had seen Erik Bruhn do the part, and he was so perfect in it, the image of him haunted me. The butler has to be introverted, reserved, with a feeling of evil. I couldn't find it in me to play this resentful, cold, and calculating individual. How do you get these qualities across in movement? For me, a performance doesn't really work unless I feel the person. When I played the butler, I felt I was emulating the character, rather than finding it inside myself to actually be him. It could have come, maybe, if I had had the chance to perform it more often, but I didn't get to do it enough to give an honest portrayal. What artistry I had to fall back on largely involved princes. Now, all of a sudden, I was playing a butler who murders someone onstage. Maybe this was taking change a little too far, too fast. It was only as I got older that I got better at this kind of character.

Naturally, I was not able to leave the classics totally behind, nor did I want to. In Berlin I danced mostly with two wonderful, very different ballerinas, Eva Evdokimova and Galina Panova. Eva was extremely analytical. You could see her think through a rehearsal or performance. She always had an expression of worry on her face, but what a dancer! She was a beautiful technician, with long limbs and extraordinary stamina. A very private individual, she was not an easy person to know. Everything was ballet, ballet, ballet. She didn't have room for much else.

Galina Panova was married to Valery Panov. The Panovs had become a *cause célèbre* in the West after they had applied to emigrate from the Soviet Union to Israel. Galina was not Jewish, but she had shown remarkable tenacity, standing with her husband through every form of duress the Soviet government could throw at them. Jail, house arrest, and an end to their performing careers were the price they paid for wanting to leave. Eventually, after twenty-seven months of various harassments, and a campaign from western ballet fans to get them released, the Soviet government let them go to Israel. Now both were in Berlin, as principal dancers.

Unlike Eva, Galina didn't think about movement, she just moved. She was a totally natural dancer, with incredible strength, and a woman who loved to laugh. Nothing was ever a problem with Galina. She didn't stop and correct herself — or anybody else for that matter. She'd just say, could we try again. We'd try again, and it would work. Galina never set out to make things perfect, she went out to dance and have a good time. You could see the Vaganova training, the very Russian style to her, particularly with the arms and back. Her arms were expansive and her upper back as straight as a board. Modern works were harder for her. She was a bit closed that way, and tended to think that, if it wasn't Russian, it wasn't worth much. When I danced *Giselle* with her, Valery came backstage afterwards to congratulate us. "Frank," he said, "you partner my wife like genius, not like me, but like genius. Incredible, in second act you run, you jump, you stay in air. You look like nothing." That was Valery's way of telling me it looked effortless.

Valery also had a great sense of humour. Like many Soviet émigrés, he was very proud of his material acquisitions, particularly his cars, a Mercedes and a Porsche Targa, which had red leather seats. We'd ride across Berlin in his Porsche, and on one occasion he had me drive. I didn't really know Berlin that well, so he was giving directions, saying, turn here, turn here, and suddenly we were on the Autobahn. No speed limit. I drove across Berlin from wall to wall, I swear, in about two and a half minutes. The last time I looked at the speedometer it was at

245 kilometres an hour, and it didn't feel as if we were going fast at all. It was amazing. "Good car, da?" he said, beaming, when we arrived home, thankfully in one piece. Valery loved his car.

Valery had choreographic ambitions. While I was in Berlin, he was working on a mammoth version of *War and Peace*. His original plan was that the ballet should run six hours, and audiences would buy tickets for consecutive days to see the show in two parts. That was Valery, totally impractical. A six-hour ballet. No one would sit still for a six-hour ballet, and the head of the Opera House said no way. So Valery gave in and made it just over three hours. Rehearsals with Galina and Valery were a little difficult because they fought as only husband and wife can. And there I was in the middle of it all. "No, Galina, no," he would say in broken English so that I could understand. "You stupid. You so stupid. Look me." Then he'd be on the floor, writhing all over. She'd get on the floor, and do *exactly* what he did. Exactly. But it was never right.

Valery's *War and Peace* was grandiose, a lot of pounding dancing, and Soviet movements with big tricks. Lifts with two hands, lifts with one hand – you felt that no hands would have been better! He spent so long working on the choreography that the administration got upset, because they had to postpone the opening so often. The ballet was eventually finished, but I never did my role of Pierre, because I didn't go back to Berlin for a second year.

I realized at the end of that first year that I had taken on too much. I hadn't thought that it would be so hard. What's to getting on a plane? I'd done that many times. But to do a year of it, with more performing than I had ever done before, that was a different story. I was exhausted. Adjusting to the time zones was the hardest part; I didn't mind the different environments. Eventually, I felt that my work was suffering.

Once, I flew overnight to Toronto from Berlin, arrived early in the morning, then took a plane on to Saskatoon to perform a school matinee in the afternoon. I arrived, did some training, got into costume and make-up. I thought, I'll just put my head down and collect some energy. I promptly fell asleep with my head down on the make-up table, only to be woken up by the on-stage call. I'd been sleeping for perhaps twenty minutes. Adrenalin rushing, I somehow got through the first act. With the intermission, the curtain came down – and everyone left the theatre! The children piled onto the school buses and away they went. They thought it was all over. Alexander Grant ran after them, shouting, "It isn't over! It isn't over!" I had flown all that way to do half a ballet. Alexander Grant was pretty upset, but secretly, I was relieved I didn't have to do the second act. I had the evening off and could rest.

I knew for sure that the travelling had become too much when suddenly, in a performance of *Fille*, my calves went into spasm, and I had to change the steps in the coda at the end of the ballet. That's when I began thinking, either I stay in one place, or I limit the amount of travelling. The decision was made for me. The next year, the director of the Opera House changed, and there was more opera, less ballet. Gert wanted me back for the same deal, but I didn't want that. I decided not to return to Berlin.

It had been a valuable year. I had learned the new choreography and new roles that I had been looking for. I really enjoyed performing more contemporary and neo-classical works, along with the classics. It was another voice for me, speaking in dance with another tone. In Berlin I got my first taste of what it meant to direct a company, and the idea of someday directing a company myself was born there. But I was glad to come home.

Ballerinas

It wasn't long after my return to the National Ballet in 1981, on a full-time basis, that I became embroiled in a nasty and very public discussion of the ballet's future – more particularly the future of its artistic director, Alexander Grant. Alexander had been heading the company for five years, and had brought in some wonderful ballets. Sir Frederick Ashton's *The Dream* and *La Fille Mal Gardée* and Maurice Béjart's *Songs of a Wayfarer* are enduring works that the company still performs. But Alexander had more recently brought in some second-rate Ashton, and many of the dancers were complaining privately that the company was adrift and without direction. There were those on the board who disagreed – they felt the company *did* have a direction, and that it was the wrong one. The National Ballet of Canada, they felt, was in danger of becoming a carbon copy of England's Royal Ballet.

With Nadia Potts, in The Sleeping Beauty, *before the perils of the pregnant fish dives.*

I was not seeing what everyone else was seeing here. Yes, I felt that we should be doing more new work and, when talking to the press, I never passed up an opportunity to say this. In May 1982, I gave an interview to the *Globe and Mail* in which I reaffirmed this, adding that I missed the excitement of the world tours we had done in the Nureyev years. I also said I felt a complacency had crept over the company, and complacency, to me, was a kind of death. This was interpreted by many as being a call for Alexander's dismissal, which it was not. I felt that Alexander was doing his best to keep the company afloat, and that he had already contributed a huge amount to its development. Box office was down, true, but who can say with any certitude, in that time of severe recession, that it had anything at all to do with Alexander? Personally, I loved Alexander's directing style, which treated us all as mature artists, in such contrast to the maternalistic regime of Celia Franca. I wondered, in brief, why we were giving this guy such a hard time.

Facing down criticism was taking its toll on Alexander. On at least one occasion, I saw him fall asleep in rehearsal. Vanessa Harwood was rehearsing for him in the studio, with Mary McDonald at the piano. I came in halfway through, ready for my own rehearsal, to find Alexander nodding off, while Vanessa was up there dancing her heart out. At the end of the solo, she looked to Alexander for comment, only to see him sound asleep. She looked at me, and then back at Alexander. Then, silently, she went and picked up her ballet bag and walked out. Mary thumped a very loud chord on the piano, which woke Alexander up with a start. You could see the steam coming from Mary's head, she was so angry. I did not have a particularly good rehearsal.

Such stories of Alexander's behaviour were rife within the company when Karen spoke out to the press on the situation. Her voice was one that everyone took very seriously, and she did not mince her words. She said she liked Alexander, but went on to roundly criticize him for his casting arrangements and complained that he had only given her one performance of *Romeo and Juliet* to dance.

What none of us knew at the time was that others had spoken privately before her. Betty Oliphant had written to the board at the time Alexander's contract came up for renewal in 1979, arguing that he not be reappointed. When the board ignored this, and reappointed him, she turned to Erik Bruhn and asked him to intervene. Betty was never one to give up easily, and was not averse to this kind of political machination. At the time Karen spoke out in May 1982, the board was reviewing the situation. Then, at the end of the following month, board chairman André Galipeault flew down to Jackson, Mississippi, where Alexander was judging a ballet competition, and told him he was fired. From the timing of our interviews, it looked very much as if Karen and I had contributed to, if not caused, Alexander's dismissal. Karen in her autobiography acknowledges that she had spoken privately to the board prior to speaking out in public, saying that she thought she had to do this for the sake of the company.

I felt at the time, and still feel, that she was wrong. I saw no particular reason for Alexander to leave. Alexander was an insightful, compassionate, and understanding man. He gave us some great ballets to dance and led us in a far more democratic way, for which we were probably not ready. He was, I think, unjustly dismissed from the company. As much as anything, he was the victim of bad timing. No artistic director, not even one of genius, would have done well at the box office in the early-eighties recession. At the time of his leaving, on the artistic side, Alexander had just acquired the rights for the National to dance John Cranko's *Onegin*. Had he been able to hang in there until the ballet was premiered, his reputation would have quickly turned around. That work, which the company owes to Alexander, was a triumph for the National, and has become another enduring part of his legacy.

Alexander decided to stay on through the following year to work out his notice at the end of the 1983 season. The dancers both admired him and disliked him for hanging in. Those were uncomfortable days.

We all knew that the board had declared they had no confidence in him, yet there he was, working with us every day. Some days, his bitterness showed, some days he was his old, optimistic self. My enduring image is of a man who was feisty, stubborn, and angry, determined to see it through to the very end, because he felt he had nothing to be ashamed of, that he had done nothing wrong. I think he was right.

~~

Shortly after coming back to the National, I began a series of guesting appearances with American ballerina Gelsey Kirkland, which were some of the most memorable in my career – and not always for good reasons. Gelsey was an amazing dancer. She had a beautiful, lyrical quality, and a way of working through movement that left the impression that she never touched the ground. It was almost as if she were floating on air, ethereal and mysterious. She had begun her career at New York City Ballet, only later to jump ship to American Ballet Theater, where for a while she enjoyed a remarkable partnership with Mikhail Baryshnikov. However, her life had recently descended into a blur of cocaine and alcohol, addictions which became serious enough that she had to cancel all her performances and go into treatment. Gelsey Kirkland by her own admission was a cocaine addict. Her problems were common knowledge in the dance world.

In November 1981, my agent, Alex Dubé – who was also Gelsey's agent – asked if I would agree to partner her. I wasn't sure whose interests he was really representing here, but he assured me that she really wanted to get back to dancing. If this were true, I was happy for her, because I was always fascinated with the way she danced, and thought we could work well together. I agreed to partner her in Italy, Miami, and Los Angeles.

First up was Italy, where we were to dance four performances of *Coppélia* in Turin. Choreographer Attillo Labiss conducted our rehearsals in French, with me doing rough-and-ready translations for Gelsey, who I was surprised to find could understand a little of the language. Labiss worked with us to adjust the choreography to suit our individual styles. From the outset, Gelsey was always questioning; I could see that she had a very analytical cast of mind, which I both enjoyed and admired. Our first two performances went without a hitch, as did the first act of the third performance, and we both felt we had done well in front of a responsive audience. Then the trouble started. Alex Dubé had come to Italy with us, acting more or less in the role of Gelsey's guardian, but he wasn't there that evening – and, without supervision, Gelsey ran wild.

At the end of the first act, as usual, I went to my dressing room, changed, and came back on stage to try some of the steps for the second act. Soon, everyone was there on stage – everyone, that is, except Gelsey. The stage manager called for her over the PA system. No Gelsey. I went downstairs looking for her, to no avail. Soon, everyone was searching. Minutes went by, and there was still no sign of her. By now, the audience was giving the slow handclap. I went back to her dressing room a second time, and there she was, in the corner behind the door, curled up in a ball, completely naked, and absolutely stoned out of her mind. I went to my room, got my gown, and took it in and covered her up, and tried to talk to her. I then ran back up to the stage manager and told him she would not be able to dance. She needed help. The stage manager called the director of the theatre – the intendant – plus the director of the ballet. Four men, with a nurse and a doctor in tow, came barging into the dressing room. Everyone was yelling and screaming, all in Italian. I didn't understand a word, but one thing was very clear: the intendant was furious.

I was standing deliberately between him and Gelsey, watching it all, and as he passed by me, the intendant barked something. Not knowing Italian, I didn't understand. "What did he say?" I asked. It seems he cursed a lot, then said, "He's big and he's strong. She can dance. Get her out on that stage. He can do it." To him, it was as simple as that. The doctor and a nurse both said, "No way, she can't perform." The theatre had to give the audience members their money back, as there was no other dancer who could perform Gelsey's role. Miraculously, in the fourth and final performance, Gelsey was fine again. But I now knew what I was in for. It was going to be a rocky ride.

I enjoyed working with Gelsey when she was clean. She was blatantly honest – Gelsey did not know any other way to be – and she was relentlessly questioning, both of herself and of anyone she was with. Everything was analysed down to the finest details. What I did was analysed, what she did was analyzed, and what we did together was analysed. Nothing escaped her relentless intelligence. Our next gig together was in Miami, and here she pulled out all the stops. The first *Giselle* we did was one of those rare and unforgettable performances, among the few that stand out in my memory. In the second act, she radiated. As I watched, she seemed transformed into the very spirit of the character. This was how I imagined Giselle to be. It was inspirational and brought out the very best in me. It was Gelsey's first American appearance in her comeback, and she received a thunderous standing ovation. Unfortunately, the performance was never repeated, and our relationship went downhill from there.

The next episode in my adventures with Gelsey came in Montreal, where we were due to tape the pas de deux from the second act of *Giselle* for a TV special on Anna Pavlova. On the first day of taping, I went to her dressing room to see how she was doing. She had been having a problem with her lower legs, which had swollen with water retention. I found her sitting on the floor examining her pointe shoes. She had cut the backs of them because her feet were so swollen. Her feet were bulbous – there was no other word for it. Despite this, she was determined to go ahead. "I'm just having a little swelling problem here, Frank," she said. "I'll see you on the set."

She did a short adagio at the beginning, and it was clear she was in pain. We decided to jump ahead to the pas de deux, and retape her solo the next day. We began working, and I was able to help by holding her on balance. We had got as far as the overhead lifts, when the director yelled cut and called me to come up to the control room. Everyone took a break while he showed me the replay. On the tape, as we did the lift, her skirt rode above her knees, and you could see that her calves were enormous, bigger than her thighs. It looked grotesque. The director asked me what we should do. I offered to change the choreography, but then it wouldn't be *Giselle*. Shooting was halted. I felt so badly for her, although I don't think anyone told her why we stopped. I certainly didn't. I think that night she tried soaking her legs to get the swelling down, but the next morning, when I arrived on set, I was told she had gone back to New York. The story was put out that she had sprained her ankle, and Marianna Tcherkassy was flown in at the last minute to dance *Giselle* with me. She was a dream to work with, a total professional, with interpretative skills to match.

My final engagement with Gelsey became a memorable non-event, one to which she curtly alludes in her memoir, *Dancing on My Grave*, with the phrase "I insulted my partner." There was rather more to it than that, and it has become something of a legend in the ballet world. Exaggerated with every retelling, it has come back to me in forms that I can barely recognize. What actually happened was this: we were scheduled to dance Ben Stevenson's *Three Preludes* in Los Angeles, at a gala fundraiser for the Los Angeles Ballet. I went down to New York to work with Gelsey, since she was to teach me the ballet. We rented a studio for the evenings, and I would arrive about five-thirty or six o'clock, do a warm-up, and be ready to start. Gelsey would usually arrive around nine o'clock, maybe nine-thirty. This went on for about two weeks, during which time I never learned the entire thing. It should have taken me only two days to learn seventeen minutes of choreography, so this was very slow going indeed. Finally, I called Patrick Bissell, a dancer with American Ballet Theater who had partnered her a lot. He knew the work, and came in the next day to work with me for a couple of hours. I finished learning the choreography in short order. Gelsey arrived just as we were wrapping up, and that was when the fun really began. I got correction after correction after correction. She was treating me as though I had no experience as a partner. I found it very demeaning. I will deal with this, I thought, but I never want to dance with her again. During the next week of rehearsal, we never once ran the ballet right through. Never.

In Los Angeles, we had a special dress-rehearsal on the day of the gala. The set was a ballet studio with a ballet barre, and a pianist on stage at the piano. We began, and the first move I had with her, I was to take her by the waist, and dead-lift her as she slid her foot along the barre. It was wrong, she said. I was doing something wrong. It was so wrong that we never got past the first eight bars. The gala was at eight o'clock, it was already six o'clock, and we still had never danced this ballet through. Again, and again, and again, we went over those first eight bars. Finally I said, "Gelsey, if you do this with your body and push like that, you'll be able to do it, and then we'll be able to get through the entire ballet, which we haven't done at all, and I would like to know what it's like to go through the entire thing without a stop."

"Fuck off," was her rather unhelpful response.

"Okay," I said. "I will." Up until that point, I felt she was worth all the effort, but at that moment, something snapped in me. I left, went to my dressing room, packed everything, and went back to my hotel, followed by my (and her) agent, Alex, and by John Clifford, the artistic director. I had called the airline and booked a flight home, when Alex and John arrived at my door, pleading with me. "I want to dance in your gala," I said, "but I cannot do it with her." When I had agreed to dance with Gelsey, one of the rules I had laid down was that she was never to use any abusive language with me or be on drugs. I had already tolerated the drugs, but I wasn't going to live with abusive language. Gelsey, I had found, boasted an amazing vocabulary.

"Do you have a Swan in your company, and does she do the White Swan pas de deux?" I asked John.

"Yes," he said.

"Can your orchestra do it?"

"Yes."

"Do you have a costume that will fit me? Then let's go back to the theatre, and I'll do White Swan with your ballerina." That settled, back at the theatre, they introduced me to my partner. She had hair down to her waist, was tanned, blonde, and very California. Need I say more. The *Baywatch* or *Sports Illustrated* magazine version of a ballet dancer. She didn't look like a classical ballerina at all, but who cared. It didn't matter; time was of the essence. We rehearsed together for twenty minutes. Without music.

I was in the dressing room, applying my make-up, when Gelsey came to the door. She stood there at the entrance, leaning on the door jamb, one hand on her hip. "Well? Are we dancing together or what?" she asked.

"No," I said. "I don't want to dance with you. We have not been through it once. I don't feel right, I don't feel safe, and I don't think I can do a credible performance."

"Oh, right," she said. And left. That was it.

I was doing a warm-up in the wings for the White Swan, and from there watched Gelsey on stage do the *Three Preludes* pas de deux *by herself.* I took three looks at it, one for each prelude. I heard the music start and looked back at the barre. I saw her with her legs around the barre, swinging back and forth like a monkey. Then she dropped down and started running around, swinging her arms. The next prelude, I turned around again, and she was bending backwards over the piano, her arms nearly touching the strings. I turned away again. The next time I looked, for the third prelude, I heard noises on the stage, and she was running around yelling "Faster, you asshole, faster" at the pianist, who was sweating beads. Her choreography consisted of bits of *Coppélia*, mixed in with bits of *Don Quixote*. It bore little resemblance to the *Three Preludes* of Ben Stevenson's creation. When the curtain came down, the audience gave sparse and questioning applause, while she mimed as though she was looking for me. Then she looked at the audience and yelled "Fuck off," before running off stage.

She picked up her suitcase, ran out of the theatre, still in costume, full make-up, and pointe shoes, across a field to where she could get a cab. She went straight to the airport, followed by her (and my) agent, and boarded a plane, still dressed in full theatrical regalia. I came on stage with my California blonde and did the White Swan pas de deux, which, considering the circumstances, went very well. As for Gelsey and me, we have only spoken a couple of times since. She is teaching, wants to lead a life out of the limelight, and has put all this behind her.

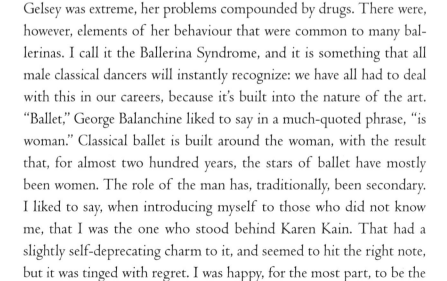

Gelsey was extreme, her problems compounded by drugs. There were, however, elements of her behaviour that were common to many ballerinas. I call it the Ballerina Syndrome, and it is something that all male classical dancers will instantly recognize: we have all had to deal with this in our careers, because it's built into the nature of the art. "Ballet," George Balanchine liked to say in a much-quoted phrase, "is woman." Classical ballet is built around the woman, with the result that, for almost two hundred years, the stars of ballet have mostly been women. The role of the man has, traditionally, been secondary. I liked to say, when introducing myself to those who did not know me, that I was the one who stood behind Karen Kain. That had a slightly self-deprecating charm to it, and seemed to hit the right note, but it was tinged with regret. I was happy, for the most part, to be the

I loved dancing Afternoon of a Faun *with Karen.*

man behind the ballerina. But I also knew that, in ballet, ballerinas –
as stars – have power, and it is a power that is conducive to abuse. It is
not uncommon for this abuse to be liberally splattered all over the
nearest unwitting object: the partner. Some personalities were more
prone to this than others, and I particularly saw it happening later in
a ballerina's life. For those affected, there seemed to be a deep-rooted
need to prove that they were never wrong. I have witnessed it over and
over again, this need to blame and make sure the world knows.

Take the case of the ballerina who, throughout a stellar career,
never really developed a partnership, and ask why. When working
with partners, she dealt with them all the same way. At the end of the
final curtain, she would immediately begin to blame her partner for
how badly the performance had gone. Why did you do this? Why
didn't you do that? You should have held me up here. Why didn't you
catch me? You were off your music. Complain, complain, complain –
usually, with the entire cast there to witness it. That was before the
curtain call. The curtain would go up, there'd be a standing ovation,
and, when the curtain came down, she would change her tune, smile,
and say you were wonderful. She needed the scapegoat. In the event of
a less-than-thunderous response, she had already made it clear that it
was someone else's fault. It gave protection in the face of a bad performance – or even the performance that was a little less than magical.
It is not so difficult for a ballerina to dominate stages, and in the
process reduce her partner to the position of *porteur*.

Ballerinas like to call themselves perfectionists, but what does this
mean for the male dancer? Working for four hours at a stretch,
without a break, trying to get it perfect, is fine if you are the one being
lifted. For the lifter, it is not so fine. It is gruelling. Perfection, in this
instance, can go hand in hand with abuse of another human being.
It is so very easy for the man in classical ballet to feel resentful,
depressed, discouraged, even vindictive, as he fights to be a worthy

partner, dancing behind the ballerina, trying to work with her to make everything move well, to display her at her best. She's the one who is doing most of the dancing, and you are there to help her make those beautiful lines, make her seem as light as air.

You can feel one of two things here: one is that you are being used, the other that you are being appreciated. Therein lies a huge difference, because if you are being appreciated, you give more, and get more back. The magic spell begins to weave itself. Truly great performances in classical ballet cannot happen without this giving. They certainly can't happen when ballerinas fall victim to the Syndrome – demanding more of others, blaming others, all in the pursuit of their own definition of perfection.

By the early 1980s, I had danced frequently with all of the National's ballerinas, aside from Karen. Veronica Tennant, Nadia Potts, Vanessa Harwood, and Mary Jago each had their moments with the Syndrome – it is almost impossible for a ballerina not to fall prey to it at some time in her career – but blessedly it was always short-lived, and very far from the extreme. I had memorable moments dancing with them all.

Veronica was easy to partner because she was so compact, though not the lightest person I ever lifted, for she had short but very dense muscles. Sometimes, she would use the great strength she had in her arms, so that taking her round in a promenade, which should have been easy, was difficult, because she was so very strong. When she was tired or nervous she would grasp your hand instead of just placing it and letting the balance work. This was the type of worker she was – full of attack. She was also courteous, very intense, and highly intelligent, and always willing to learn, with a good solid technique and an open mind. Of all the National's ballerinas, she was the most intellectual, and to me had the feeling of a learned rather than a natural artist. Veronica was a dancer who liked to calculate things. She would

Romeo and Juliet, *my favourite ballet with Veronica.*

always block and count the number of steps. She once said that she was a very clumsy person, an odd thing for a dancer to say, but when she said it, I suddenly understood why she seemed so careful.

She and I did a wonderful *Romeo and Juliet* at Artpark in Lewiston, New York. It was one of those special moments when everything clicked. She was replacing Karen at the last minute, and, as is often the case, the replacement performance was one of the best, because there was no time to get nervous or think too much. You are going on pure instinct. Often with Veronica, her drive to succeed meant that she applied too much gasoline instead of just enough to go, and this would sometimes cloud our attempt at unity, but on this occasion, she really relaxed into the role. To me, she also seemed to be transformed by a series of performances with British dancer Anthony Dowell in *The Dream*. These were just filled with abandon, and I'd never seen her that way before. It came from the soul and the heart. It felt like she had taken a huge step towards becoming a natural artist, because she had proven to herself that she had this naturalness within her. With Anthony, she forgot about herself and gave and gave, and so did he, because that was the way he knew. Our *Romeo and Juliet* came after this, and it seemed as if I were dancing with a different person. She was more conscious of everything around her, rather than being turned in on herself. As a result, she became infinitely more potent as a performer. It was wonderful to see.

Vanessa Harwood could not have approached things more differently. With her, it was always casual, a let's-see-what's-going-to-happen attitude. Nerves never got the better of Vanessa. She enjoyed performances. Bubbly, enthusiastic, easy-going, she was a delight to dance with and be around, a woman with a wicked laugh. Nothing was so important to Vanessa that it was worth getting upset about. It was "We'll do it. It'll happen. It'll be there." Her strength was her natural ability — she had such a flexible body, and a good, if soft, gentle technique. She

With Vanessa Harwood, at the gala where our
Le Corsair *pas de deux brought the house down.*

had an extraordinary sense of balance and was an excellent turner, with great stamina on stage, and a very sexual presence. For me, when I saw her dancing, I wished there was more rapidity and sharpness in her legs, but that was a minor thing. Sometimes Vanessa was a little shy of the music, but that was how she heard it, and it became a trademark that worked for her – and for her audience.

One of the great performances I did with Vanessa was that old warhorse of a pas de deux that is brought out at every gala, *Le Corsair*. This is a very scary pas de deux, and Vanessa approached it with such ease. The main reason it worked so well all came down to this easy-going attitude of hers. She added a dimension of calmness to what was, for me, a high-anxiety evening. That was the mode she worked in. I was ready to go, as you have to be before *Corsair* starts, for you enter the stage running, with your heart pounding. That's the intensity that piece requires of the male dancer. On this occasion, we just powered our way through the thing with great energy, but also great ease. There was an explosion from the audience at the end. There are still people who to this day remember that performance. It was not without risk, but the risks paid off.

Nadia Potts was different again. She was highly strung – not on the surface, but you sensed with her that there was an internal nervousness, almost amounting to fear. It rarely showed on her face, but I think she had a knot inside her all the time.

Nadia had a beautiful body and face, good feet, and was extremely strong and very well schooled. Nadia's movements were always very clean. She never went too far, she always went to precisely the right place, never over the top. Nadia was textbook in style, which I think she felt she had to be. She was under additional pressure because her mother was one of the teachers at the school.

Nadia gave me one of the worst frights of my dancing career. We were to dance *The Sleeping Beauty* together, and I was really looking forward to the performance. Just before the curtain went up, we were on stage, practising a few things, when she said in an off-hand way, "I hope I don't feel too heavy. I'm putting on a little weight. I'm pregnant." All I could think of was all the partnering I had to do around her waist. Those fish dives, where I had to grab her around her belly and hold her upside-down.

"You're pregnant," I said, stunned. "And you're dancing?"

"Yes," she said calmly. "The doctor said it's fine."

Well, it may have been fine for the doctor, but it wasn't fine with me. I could feel my face growing white from the shock, although you couldn't tell from my Max Factor Tan No. 2.

I went rushing down to the pit to see her husband, Harold Gomez, who played clarinet in the orchestra. Musicians never see dancers in costume in the pit five minutes before a performance, and I heard them giggling. "Harold, do you know your wife is pregnant?" I stupidly blurted out. This was hardly news to Harold; he had known for a couple of months. "But I have to partner her," I wailed. What if something went wrong, and I was the cause? Harold was perfectly calm but I was plain terrified. I was also annoyed at her timing. There surely were better times to make this announcement than five minutes before a performance. Nadia glided through the performance with an esprit that I was only aware of once it was all over. She seemed to be enjoying the show. As for me, it was the most careful performance I've ever done in my life. I have handled eggs more roughly. Partner her by the tutu, I thought, anything to avoid the waist. When it came to the fish dives, I whispered after every one, "Are you okay?" "Yes," she hissed each time, wondering what all the fuss was about.

I always had a soft spot for Mary Jago, who was one of my very first partners, and who had been kindness and generosity itself to a very inexperienced young man. There was a short period of time during which I was very enamoured of her, although she was dating the stage

The magic lift from Don Juan. *The apparently levitated
ballerina is Mary Jago, one of my favourite partners.*

manager of the company at the time. I was about seventeen or eighteen, and she was in her twenties, which then seemed a huge age gap. It
was obvious she really liked me too, but we left it at that. Of all the
ballerinas in the company, I danced with Mary the least — more by
default than by choice. I danced Romeo to her first Juliet, and we did
a remarkable White Swan pas de deux accompanied by the Toronto
symphony, but the ballet I enjoyed doing most with her was *Don Juan.*
She really excelled as the Lady in White, or messenger of death, and
whenever we did the ballet together, she was always able to bring out
more emotion in me.

This emotional connection is what you are looking for on stage.
Without it, the dance remains technical and dry. Royal Winnipeg ballerina Evelyn Hart, who could be very difficult to work with in the
studio, was always able to bring feeling to the stage and draw more
feeling out of me, though it wasn't always easy working with her. She
came to dance with the National fairly late in her career, long after she
had made her reputation with the Royal Winnipeg, and after her
triumph in a Norbert Vesak piece, *Belong.* A modern work, this had
become a trademark for her, but Evelyn really wanted to get away from
it and show that she could do more. I was scheduled to partner her in
her first *Giselle,* which would also be her first guest performance with the
National Ballet. Working with Evelyn when she didn't know a role was
easier than when she did. When she was learning, she was very understanding, and there would be a good exchange of ideas on how to do
things. Once she felt she had mastered a role, everything changed.
There was no longer any recognition that anyone else had anything to
say about what was going to happen on that stage. Only what she
was feeling, and what was coming out of her body, was important. If
she asked for something, it wasn't a request any more, it was a demand.
Yet, once on stage, dancing with Evelyn was a joy, an absolute joy.

In our first *Giselle*, Evelyn got into a panic early in the first act. "Frank," she said, as we were miming conversation, "my shoe is untied. What shall I do?" What did she expect me to say?

"Do it up," I replied, wondering if she was thinking of dancing her solo with her ribbons trailing around her feet. First performances can induce that kind of panic, and we howled about it afterwards, but at the time, to her, it wasn't at all funny. I stood in front of her while she tied the ribbon, miming conversation to my sidekick, Wilfrid, to distract the audience. The rest of the performance went without a hitch. The next day, the *Globe and Mail* said that Evelyn had "stolen the entire winter season." New York critic Anna Kisselgoff, who had flown in to view the performance, announced that Canadian ballet had a new heroine.

Evelyn became a frequent guest with the National, and during that time I got to know her quite well. She later wrote that she had fallen in love with me. I had no idea at the time. I was someone she could talk to and laugh with (she has a great sense of humour) and there was an attraction in that. I liked being with her, and we hung out together a fair bit during those years and did the odd tour together. I have a memory of Evelyn checking into hotels, and instantly heading off shopping, to the nearest mall. She is a great shopper. I always thought it was something very primitive about her, that wherever she went, she had to forage and gather.

Over the years, I have danced with these and many other ballerinas. In the course of time, I developed Frank's List of Do's and Don'ts for Ballerinas. There isn't an item on it that other male partners would not subscribe to:

1. Don't piqué onto your partner's foot. Toe shoes are very hard, like steel, and can cause a lot of damage.

2. Make sure in a pirouette in retiré to overcross your leg. This reduces the chance of hitting your partner where he least wants to be hit.

3. Don't put on too much weight. A touchy subject, this, given ballerinas' tendencies towards anorexia. But the reality is, with the lifts that are now an integral part of ballet, there is a maximum weight a partner can be expected to haul. The figure can vary, but for me it was around 115 pounds. More than that was too much. If you are being partnered by a flatbed truck, a real lumberjack-type of guy, fine, you can be heavier.

4. Tape all rings on your fingers, because you can slash your partner, especially with multi-karat diamonds. I've seen blood dripping from slash cuts across a partner's chest. It is not a pretty sight.

5. Whenever possible, don't announce your pregnancy five minutes before the performance. This will save your partner an anxiety attack.

6. Make bobby pins secure and coat them with hairspray. This will prevent them flying out and blinding your partner.

7. Don't have a short high fifth with elbows sticking out. That way you won't break your partner's nose, as Karen did mine.

8. Don't jump into your partner's arms if he isn't looking. This can be dangerous, for both of you.

9. Be as much the image of a princess as possible. Be on balance at all times. Be strong, be in shape, be technically proficient. Be perfect.

10. Flatter your partner at every opportunity you have. Tell him how great he is, how wonderful, how much you need him, and that without him nothing is possible. Insecure males in a female world, we need our egos boosted.

If at least some of these injunctions had been obeyed, I would have avoided a dislocated shoulder (Gelsey Kirkland), a broken nose (Karen

Kain), a broken finger (Karen Kain), bruised metatarsals (Nadia Potts), and a compressed disc (Carla Fracci). There would have been no way to avoid the general wear and tear on the back that comes from lifting (every ballerina I ever danced with). It may all sound a little grim, but, in truth, I wouldn't have missed a moment of it.

CHAPTER
12

How I Met My Wife

In November 1982, I got a phone call from my friend Howard Marcus. Howard had been a dancer with the company and was now running his own business as an interior designer. He wanted me to meet his friend Erene Christopher, a marketing manager for Elizabeth Arden's cosmetics, who had a sponsorship proposal for me. Howard was something of an entrepreneur, and I think he saw himself as my agent.

We were mounting a new *Don Quixote*, and the only time I had free was after dress rehearsal on a Tuesday night at around eleven-thirty, so we arranged to meet then. I had a miserable dress rehearsal, in which everything went wrong. There were so many things to work through, and very little time to do it, because the opening night was the next day. I left the theatre wondering how I was going to get it right in time. The last thing I wanted was a business meeting. Little

Our official engagement portrait.

did I know that, at the time, Erene had the flu, and she wanted to be there about as much as I did. We went to the Old Fish Market, where I ate, and Erene explained the project.

She thought it would be a good idea to have me sponsor one of Elizabeth Arden's men's fragrances, as my name was then well known. She gave me bottles of Lagerfeld for Men and Burberry, and I unscrewed the tops and smelled them. I hated the Lagerfeld but thought that, if I wore a fragrance, I could wear the Burberry. To me, uncommercial as I was, it actually mattered that I liked what I sponsored. Earlier, I had turned down Coca-Cola because I didn't drink it. I also didn't look at my career as having any promotional value. I was a dancer, and wanted recognition as such. I didn't want to be recognized more for doing Coca-Cola ads.

Erene's deal really wasn't important to me at all, but she intrigued me. Her manner was so direct, but also sensitive. I was far less interested in her fragrances than in her. I agreed in principal to sponsor the Burberry, and we wrapped up the evening fairly quickly. I went home to worry about *Don Quixote*, which premiered the next day with most of the problems miraculously disappearing.

Erene and I talked a couple of times about the promotion project. Then she called a few times to invite me out. It was only on the third occasion, she says, that I finally got the message. The invitation was to a birthday party, which she was throwing for her sister-in-law Karen. It was on a Wednesday, so I went after the performance. I felt wonderful because we were doing *Songs of a Wayfarer* – Tomas Schramek and I always enjoyed performing the work, and this time we had received a standing ovation. I arrived at the party in high spirits, bringing a bottle of champagne. I gave this to Erene, telling her to remember never to drink it alone. It was a thoroughly enjoyable evening, and I didn't want to leave.

I continued to meet Erene. At first it was to discuss the deal, but this quickly fell apart when Erene left Elizabeth Arden. That out of the way, we went on meeting as friends. From the very start, I really liked her. Erene had seen me perform, but I never got a sense from her that she presumed to know me in person, as is quite often the case. That liking quickly developed into love.

Erene was born in Cyprus, but grew up in the United States. From the start, I loved her dynamism and self-assurance, her openness and honesty, and above all I loved her laugh. She has a great sense of humour. Erene has what I can only describe as a sense of wellness about her, and a sensitive, extremely intuitive, side that also really attracted me. All this shone through at once. Early-evening meetings at the Bellair Café became more and more frequent. She came to visit me when I was performing in London, Ontario, and met me backstage in the dressing room that I shared with Tomas Schramek and Raymond Smith. She walked in as we three were sitting there, half made-up and less than half dressed. Erene, in a full-length, long-haired fox coat stood looking gorgeous – and slightly embarrassed. "Wow, who was that?" they asked after she had left. I was bursting with pride.

Our relationship was very intense from the beginning. We could talk about anything and everything, and when she drank that bottle of champagne I had brought her that birthday night, she drank it with me. I knew I was in love when, before a difficult performance, when I was particularly nervous and apprehensive, she turned to me and said, "Well, don't worry, I'm here. I'll always be here." That made me feel complete, knowing that there was someone there for me. It was a simple thing, yet, said at exactly the right time, it meant so much.

After a few months I wanted Erene to see my house, because my intention was that we would live together there. I owned my house and she was renting, so that seemed to make sense. There was one little problem in all this. I may have owned a house, but I had virtually no furniture. You have to picture this. The living room and dining room were empty, there was a table and four chairs in the kitchen. A couch and a black vinyl beanbag chair in an upstairs bedroom. That was about it. No pictures. Nothing. No kitchen utensils to speak of. A frying pan, a fork, a knife, and one pot to boil water. I decided to invest a lot of money ripping out the gaudy carpets, redoing the floors, buying furniture – making it a home. I didn't want her to come anywhere near before I did this. So, I spent the necessary cash. Fast. Soon there were chairs, a furnished living room, a semblance of a dining room, more pots. It set me back a few thousand dollars, which I couldn't afford at the time.

I proudly brought her back to show her the home, hoping that she would like it, but things didn't quite go the way I had planned. First off, we hadn't had dinner, so Erene said she would make us something. She went to the fridge, only to find some old food with green fuzz on it. Not quite the impression I had hoped to make. It was all inedible, so we gave up the idea of eating and just sat and talked. Then, when Erene went upstairs to the bathroom, she quickly came rushing back down. "You have to open the door next to the bathroom," she said. "You've closed spirits in there, and it's too crowded for them." I had gone to all this trouble to make the house seem habitable, but it didn't matter what I had done, or how much of a home I had made. The house had ghosts. Erene even pointed out the exact spots where the ghosts were. There was one in the upstairs back bedroom and also one in the living room. To make matters worse, the ghost in the back bedroom was not a nice one.

I was stunned. I really liked my house, and didn't think there was anything bad in it. But I decided to find a spiritualist who would come to the house and find out what exactly was there. Karen pitched in and helped me track one down. The spiritualist met us both at the house; he knew why he was asked to come, but not the exact details. A tall man in his late thirties, with black curly hair, he walked into the home, looked around, and pointed to the same spots where Erene had felt there were ghosts. Exactly the same places. He even described the ghosts: in the living room, there was an old man, content but possessive, and this was his spot. He didn't want to leave. Upstairs, he felt the presence of children with hands around their necks, as if being suffocated. The spiritualist told us the spirits were not danger-ous. He just recommended that we occupy the home and help them pass on. Erene seemed to understand this concept. Clearly, Erene had a psychic talent, and it spooked me a bit. Erene moved in, we began occupying the rooms, and the spirits left.

Erene was the first woman I had lived with, and it took me a while to get used to domesticity. For one thing, I was an absolutely clueless cook. I hated cooking because of all the standing — it was only as I eased off dancing that I later came to enjoy it. I could boil an egg, and once I tried to fry a turkey — it took three hours, and I burned all the Shake 'n' Bake. I learned by working with Erene and watching her. It was a slow process. When guests came for dinner, my idea of helping, before I became a fully trained sous-chef, was to go out and wash the car. "What are you doing?" Erene asked the first and last time I did this. "I'm washing the car," I replied. "It's got to be clean, hasn't it?"

Things were running along smoothly, and I thought I was getting pretty good at sous-chefing, when I was firmly put in my place. Guests were about to arrive, the tension was mounting, and, as usual, there were too many things still to be done. Erene needed lemon juice, and asked me to squeeze a lemon. I stood there, in the kitchen, liter-ally squeezing a lemon. "What are you doing?" she asked with an irri-tated look. She had to tell me to cut it and juice it. "I suppose if I told you to separate two eggs, you'd put one at one end of the kitchen, and the other at the other end," she said. As a husband-in-training, I still had a lot to learn. Eventually, I got to the point where I'd attempt a simple meal. People now say I'm a good cook. I wouldn't go that far. I know some basic rules and can read a recipe, that's all.

We had been living together for about a year when, on a January winter afternoon, I was outside in the snow, shovelling the sidewalk.

Erene was upstairs having a shower. As I was shovelling the snow, I told myself that, if I could hit a tree with a snowball three times, then today would be the day I would ask her to marry me. I stood on the sidewalk and made the snowballs. I threw them, and hit the tree each time. I came inside, and Erene was walking out of the shower, dripping wet. I asked her to marry me. "The way I look?" she said. "Yes, the way you look. I want us to be married." Why snowballs on a tree when it was such an important decision? I hoped I wouldn't hit the tree, that I wouldn't have to do it, at the same time knowing that I wanted to do it. I know, even if I had missed, I would have asked her.

I took Erene home to meet my parents, wanting her to see who my people were. My father was very tense, and my mother spent most of the time in the kitchen. Only my brother, Peter, behaved normally. My father, after he realized Erene was a vegetarian, kept offering her plates of meat. Then he would bring up my old girlfriends. "What happened to Hilary?" he asked. "And what happened to that other girl you liked? What was her name, Sabina?" This was turning into a nightmare visit, and I don't think he even knew what he was doing. My father had begun to hate Erene over the phone, from the minute when I first told him about her. This without even knowing her. He had always talked to me about how I should eventually, as he liked to say, plant a family. He saw it as a search. He would help me find not so much a woman, as a vessel for my children.

My father wanted to be involved in all the important decisions of my life. I had chosen a career he did not like, one that had his active disapproval. I had bought a car without his help — that was bad enough. I bought a house on my own — that was worse. Now I had made the most important decision of all without him. It was very clear to everyone that day that Erene was not welcome. He thought she was a gold-digger, after me for my money. He asked her bluntly how much money she made, and was more than a little taken aback at the amount. I was upset. I had hoped for recognition that she was an important person in my life. Failing that, I hoped for at least an understanding that it might be important to get along with Erene because she was going to be around for some time. Instead, I got nothing but hostility. To my father, Erene was always "that wife of Frank's."

Erene is Greek Orthodox, and we decided we wanted a religious ceremony. That meant that I had to be baptized. I went through the Orthodox service, replete with godparents, decked out in a rather skimpy bathing suit, as water was splashed all over me. We had a marriage-preparation session of about forty-five minutes with a priest, who talked about God, the sacraments, the importance and meaning of marriage. Then he turned to Erene. "If Frank, your future husband, should stray, you should forgive him, but if you should stray . . ." He never finished the sentence. He didn't have to. It was clear that, for the wife, there was no forgiveness. We were both dumbfounded, and knew that if we so much as glanced at each other, we would only start laughing. That would have been a bad mistake. We needed his double dispensation to marry outdoors and during the Lenten period for the Virgin Mary. He then asked if I had any questions. I said that I didn't. "But after we get married," I said, "I know that, if we ever have any problems, we can come to you for help." Erene looked first at him, and then at me. She said nothing.

The ceremony took place in August 1983, in the glorious garden of Linda Maybarduk and her husband, Bill Alguire. Dancer Jeff Hyslop, whom I had met taping a CBC special about Karen, was my best man. Jeff and I drove to Linda's house in my friend Victor Melnikoff's 1953 Jaguar, with a chauffeur who felt he needed to pack a gun to protect the car. It was a hot day, there was no air-conditioning in the Jag, and the traffic on the Queen Elizabeth Way was moving at a snail's pace. Caught up among baseball fans and CNE and Ontario Place visitors, we were sure that we would be late. We got there just in time — well, I suppose they could hardly have started without me — and, once there, all my anxiety melted away. We were surrounded by

Our wedding.

friends, including many people from the National Ballet. Even my father was there, though it had taken me days to convince him to come to the wedding. I truly wanted him to be there, to be part of it all, but he kept saying that he would not come. It was only on the morning of the wedding that I was finally able to persuade him. When I got up to speak at the reception after the ceremony, I saw my father out of the corner of my eye, standing up as if to speak for me, and my mother, a worried look on her face, pulling him back down.

CHAPTER
——————
1 3

Last Years at the National

With the dismissal of Alexander Grant in June 1982, the search for a new artistic director for the National Ballet began. The head of the search committee called me one evening, as he did the other principal dancers, to ask my opinion on the candidates. Erik Bruhn was the clear favourite, and I said I thought he would be an excellent director for the company, one that would add to its reputation. Like most of the dancers, I felt it would be an incredible honour if he would take on the job. Erik agreed, and arrived to take over the company in the late summer of 1983.

Erik Bruhn was no stranger to Toronto. In the 1970s, he had come over to restage *La Sylphide*, to create *Coppélia*, and to oversee his version of *Swan Lake*. I worked with him on each of these ballets. At the point at which I got to know him, Erik's *danseur noble* days were over. He had

——————

As Onegin, in John Cranko's ballet.

retired from the principal classical roles at the age of forty-three, suffering from pains that were only much later diagnosed as an ulcer. He was now working as a director and restager, occasionally lighting up the stage with some very memorable performances as a character artist. He had always been more of a dancer's dancer, a man who many felt never had the public recognition he deserved. Although his style was completely different, he was a dancer who could challenge his close friend Nureyev. He was, however, definitely eclipsed by Rudolf, and there may have been some resentment. Rudolf, after all, was younger and in high demand. Where Rudolf was emotional, flamboyant and open, Erik was intellectual, restrained, and guarded. I think there were a lot of unresolved issues there. Unlike Rudolf, Erik was never open about his sexuality.

He would come for dinner at Karen's quite frequently, and it was here that I got to know him a little better. In the 1970s, Karen's apartment at Broadview and Danforth almost seemed like my home, for we were together most of the time. She would invite Erik over, sometimes alone, sometimes with others, and would memorably burn the food. Her signature dish was lasagna. She wasn't a cook — I wasn't a cook then, either, so perhaps I shouldn't talk — but it was wonderful to have Erik there, in the living room, and to listen to his tales. Mostly, he loved to tell funny stories about other dancers, often at their expense. Sarcastic and sardonic, he enjoyed laughing at his own jokes and his own cleverness. I was in awe of him, but I always had a very uneasy feeling around him socially. Partly it came from being so much younger, and viewing him as this god of dance, but it was more than that. He was so clever, so ingenious, with such a biting tongue, that when he talked incisively about other people, it always made me wonder what he might be saying about me if I weren't in the room.

Karen, Erik, and I performed on stage together in Erik's production of *Coppélia* in the late 1970s. *Coppélia* is a comedy, and is usually seen as a children's ballet. In most productions it is primarily the story of

Franz and Swanhilda, in which Franz becomes besotted with a life-like doll built by Dr. Coppélius. Erik's version was different. The plot emphasis shifted to give the character of Dr. Coppélius almost equal weight, and the tone of the ballet was far darker, with more nuance than you might find elsewhere. That was particularly the case when Erik played Dr. Coppélius. I knew very well the power that Erik had on stage. Just gazing into his eyes, even for a moment, you knew what he could do. You could see he truly believed in the person he was – and more than that, revelled in it. *Coppélia*, with Erik in it, ceased to be a children's story, and became something quite serious and frightening. When Erik was Coppélius, you really felt that he believed he could create life itself.

Now Erik had the National Ballet of Canada on which to exercise his considerable creative powers. There was an immediate re-energizing of the company when he arrived. Morale lifted one-hundred-fold. Erik had a commanding presence when he walked into a room. With his deep bass voice, his blond good looks, and that sense of aloofness that he made work so well for him, he had a natural authority. Of course, it didn't hurt that we all knew he was one of the greatest male dancers the world had ever seen. Now he was here – directing the company, giving class. Erik Bruhn, with his lines, his gorgeous lines and impeccable taste, was giving class. Maybe some of the look, the taste, and the knowledge would get passed on. I was hopeful.

Erik's character was written on his class. He was always very clear, but what he gave us to do was very difficult. The combinations were intricate, entertaining mind-twisters – the more intricate and difficult they were, the more he got a kick out of seeing us take on the challenge. More often than not, we would collapse in confusion, but it was all great fun. Erik, the mad inventor, the real-life Dr. Coppélius, was inventing things just to see if we could do them. The one problem with all this was that I never felt physically prepared after his

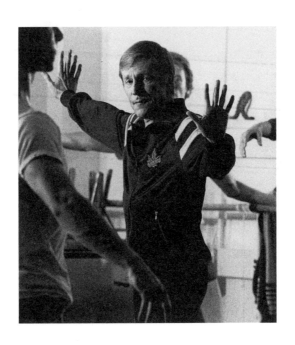

Above: Erik Bruhn taking class.

Below: Alexander in the studio, shortly before his departure.

class, or that I had worked all my muscles in the way they should be worked. Class with Erik had an abstract, intellectual quality to it. I didn't always feel it readied me for the next six or eight hours of work.

One of the first things Erik did on his arrival was call a meeting of all the departments to lay out his plans. When he gathered the principal dancers together, he let us know he was going to be making changes, and that there were people within the company whose contracts he would not renew. He mentioned names, but since none of the names were among our privileged group of principals, I assumed that this did not apply to us. At the same time, Erik asked for our support. Those of us with guesting engagements were asked to reduce the load. As Karen and I were doing the bulk of the guesting, it seemed clear to me that he wanted and needed us to be around. Yes, Erik wanted to build and change the company, bring in new choreography, and develop the younger dancers. To me, that didn't mean that he didn't want us. Karen felt that we were all being put on notice, but I didn't get that impression at all. I came away from the meeting with a good feeling. Erik had said he needed our help and support.

It was clear that Erik was in command. Seeing him in action, far from making me feel nervous, as it did some other dancers, gave me a sense of security. He left the impression that he knew exactly where he wanted to go, and such a sense of purpose was invigorating. Erik didn't want the National to be the same as any other company. Gone were the days of trying to emulate other big companies, such as the Royal. Instead of harking back to the past, Erik was determined to push the company into the future and create something with a unique identity.

Change was on show from the first gala he organized in February, 1984. It began in informal style with a class on stage. Erik, a microphone in hand, took us all through our paces. Audiences and dancers alike got a sense that something new was happening. The program was quite unlike any other gala we had done — full of works by young choreographers, including Danny Grossman, David Earle, and my old school friend, Robert Desrosiers, who later went on to choreograph *Blue Snake* for Erik. Karen and I led the company at the end of the evening in the final act of *Sleeping Beauty*, a reminder that the classics were still an integral part of the National's repertoire.

During the first year of Erik's regime, in May 1984, we premiered John Cranko's *Onegin*, which gave the company ballerinas a marvellous, dramatic role in the heroine, Tatiana. For me, it was the chance to portray the title role, Onegin – a difficult part, which I was able to get a grip on only after much struggle. There were technical challenges to the role: some of the lifts were extremely difficult, and the turns in arabesque and attitude of the first solo were never a strength of mine. Stamina was also a factor. The technical challenges were hard enough, but what I really found difficult was coming to grips with the character. Onegin is a dark, romantic charmer, a playboy who toys with Tatiana, only to discover at the end of the ballet that he loves her. The discovery comes too late. In a final pas de deux that is wild with conflicting emotions, Tatiana rejects him.

Emotionally, I was hard-pressed to find the motivation for Onegin's change in character. It was also difficult to get the right balance of feelings. I wanted to present a man who was cold and uncaring, without making him too unlikeable. I had to work on finding him within myself, and then to translate that coldness and lack of caring into the movement. The interesting thing was that, the more I found him, the easier the movements became. I suddenly understood just how thoroughly Cranko understood what he was doing. The role became something of an obsession with me. Erene said that I lived him. "I don't know who you are any more," she would say. "You're becoming him." I was very worried about this role. I wasn't at all sure I could find him, which was made worse for me because I had such a great respect for Cranko's choreography. The one part of the ballet that was easy for me was the "mirror" pas de deux, where Onegin becomes everything that Tatiana has imagined and wants him to be. Switching back to the cold and rather lost person that he is in reality was always harder.

Reid Anderson, then a principal dancer with the Stuttgart Ballet, came over to stage the work, and to dance it with Karen. I partnered Sabina Allemann, one of the company's younger ballerinas whose career was on the rise. It was the first time I had not danced a major role with Karen, and we never did do the ballet together, but dancing with Sabina was a pleasure. Sabina wanted everything to be right, and if it wasn't right, we would do it again and again until it was. She had incredible drive, and when we got into the studio, we got right down to making the thing happen. I had a few problems with some of the details of the choreography, where the action seemed to be at odds with the character, but these were minor. Generally, Cranko had a way of making the steps say dramatically exactly what he wanted said, and the choreography blended exquisitely with music. The last pas de deux is one of the best-choreographed pas de deux that he ever did. There is nothing extraneous in it – it comes right to the point. If I had troubles with the character, I always loved the dancing in this ballet.

I was enormously happy one day when, after a performance, Erik put his head around the door of the dressing room and said, "Good, Frank, just keep doing what you are doing." That may not sound like much, but to me it was the equivalent of high praise. I believed he meant that my performance was on the right track, which is what any artist wants to hear from an artistic director. But was that what he really meant? Erik was not one to say what he did not mean, but he could balance words carefully in an enigmatic way. He once told me how he handled talking to dancers after really awful performances: he would go backstage and say something that could be interpreted any way, along the lines of "That was incredible. I've never seen anything like it." Those who wanted to could take this as a compliment. "Just keep doing it." Surely, this was not ambiguous. You could hardly say

With Sabina Allemann, in Onegin.

that about a performance you hated. But I had to think about what he meant. That's the way it was with Erik. You had to mull over everything he said very carefully.

During that first year, Erik made himself available to us all. He was a presence in the studio, and I always felt I could go and talk to him. He would take the time, he didn't close the door on you, but his answers were often opaque. Even more often, there was no answer at all, even if he talked to you for twenty minutes. You would think about what he said, puzzle over it afterwards, and wonder, What on earth did he mean? If his answer to a question were overly long, you knew that he hadn't made up his mind yet. Usually, if you asked him a question, he would say yes or no instantly. And that would be that. When he had made up his mind, Erik was very direct.

At the end of his first year with the company, in 1984, Erik made some radical changes in personnel. From this, it became clear that Karen — who had felt we were all on notice — was right. Of the principals, Mary Jago retired as she had planned, while Nadia Potts and Vanessa Harwood left more reluctantly. Other dancers, seeing the writing on the wall, left the company before being asked to go. I understood that Erik could be ruthless when he felt that it was necessary for his vision of the company. He held a second meeting of the principal dancers, and unlike the first meeting when he had encouraged us to be there in support, in this second meeting, he suggested we take whatever guesting engagements came up. He wanted to make opportunities for the enormously talented roster of young dancers that had graduated into the company from the school — Sabina Allemann, Kimberly Glasco, Martine Lamy, Kevin Pugh, Owen Montagu, Jeremy Ransom, and Rex Harrington, to name a few.

I took Erik's injunction seriously, and set about looking for other work. I also had hints, at this stage, that Erik was less than pleased with my dancing, although he never said anything directly to my face about it. Rumours are rife in a ballet company, which is a small place, and I had heard in a roundabout way that Erik believed I was lazy and unreliable. It even came back to me that he thought I should not be partnering Karen and had told Karen to find another partner. This was devastating. I had no idea Erik was saying these things, and I was enormously hurt. In fact, I later found out he wasn't saying them, but by then it was too late. Years later, Karen told me what he had really said. Erik suggested that she should do her own performance and not see her work in relation to mine. Her career, he added, was not tied inextricably to mine. But I did not know that then, and I did not do then what I should have done – go to Erik and ask him if it were true, was this what he really thought? Instead, I worried silently. Practically, I decided that, if this were Erik's opinion of me, I couldn't be sure how much I figured in his vision for the future, although for the time being I had no reason to worry. My three-year contract gave me a minimum of thirty-five performances for 1984–85. Still, I felt I needed to look around for other outside engagements.

That summer, I got involved in a Canadian feature film, my first and last such venture. Producer Robert Lantos and director Lewis Furey were casting *Night Magic*, a bizarre operetta with music by Furey and lyrics by Leonard Cohen. They were looking for two male principal dancers, and I thought, why not? On paper, at least, the project looked good, and my co-dancer was an enormously talented member of Eddy Toussaint's Montreal company, Louis Robitaille. Carole Laure and Nick Mancuso were the stars, and there was a strange linking role in the film for the great French film actress, Stéphane Audran. Eddy Toussaint did the choreography. This production had a wealth of talent attached to it. It even had a few memorable songs. What it lacked was a coherent script. I spent about ten days on set, in the old National Theatre in Montreal, where the air was clouded with dense smoke most of the time. At the end of the shoot, I had to get my contact lenses replaced, since they had been ruined by all the oil-based smoke. When I look at the film today, I find it hard to see what any of us could have been thinking. It certainly did nothing for any of our careers, and is now relegated to the dusty bottom shelves of specialty video stores.

On a more serious career track, I looked around to see what other opportunities there were for me as a principal dancer. Boston Ballet was looking for a male principal, and it seemed to be a good fit. It was then a regional company, with some rather tired, second-rate productions in its repertoire, although the quality of the dancing was good. Boston had the benefit of being close. I could get down there for a rehearsal and return the same day, in the same time zone, so the problems of the Berlin jet lag would not arise. The deal was signed, and a schedule agreed upon by the National and Boston, in which the National got first choice of dates. I would split my time between Toronto, where I was still a principal dancer, and Boston, where I was resident guest artist.

If it were true that Erik was less than pleased with me, this new arrangement started out on a wrong note that would have aggravated him even further. The paperwork had not yet been completed and my contracts with the National and Boston had not yet been signed, although schedules had been exchanged, when, somewhere along the line, someone goofed. I was scheduled by the National for a performance in St. John's, Newfoundland. The National had not checked my Boston schedule, and therefore I was down for a performance that I could not have done – I had already left for Boston. Erik was furious when he realized I was not there. "He's not here. Fire him," he said to Bob Johnston, the company manager. "Well," said Bob, "we can't actually fire him, because we haven't hired him yet." Erik, in a quieter voice, replied, "Well, hire him, and then fire him." Part of the reason Erik was so furious was that he had been told that people in St. John's were extremely touchy about performers not making shows there.

They wanted Kain and Augustyn in *Coppélia*, they had been told they would get Kain and Augustyn, and now Augustyn wasn't showing up. Erik never normally lost his cool, but this time he was angry – and unfortunately angry at me. Later, I apologized to him for the mix-up, but he brushed it off as being of no importance.

Schedules sorted, for the next few years my dancing life was divided between Toronto and Boston. I took a small apartment on Commonwealth Avenue, in an old brownstone, and Erene, who was now working for Max Factor, would fly down to spend weekends with me. Despite my uncertainty about Erik, this was one of the happiest times of my life. We were newly married and very much in love. I would do crazy things to welcome her. On her birthday, shortly after she had told me she was pregnant, I bought thirty or forty balloons and spent the morning blowing them up and scattering them around the apartment. I then left for rehearsal, so that Erene arrived to find an apartment full of balloons, along with a big fluffy toy rabbit, which she named Boston Barley.

Boston Ballet's studios and theatre were on the edge of an area known as the Combat Zone. The first time I walked to the theatre, women standing around on the street asked how I was, and, totally absorbed in my own little world, I didn't realize they were hookers. "They're really friendly around here," I said when I arrived at the theatre. The other dancers looked at me as if to say, "Gee, Frank, don't they have hookers in Toronto?" I was always at my most anxious on the way to the theatre before a performance, so it didn't surprise me that I was this unaware, but I was still a bit embarrassed.

The repertoire I danced in Boston was mostly classical – *Giselle*, *The Nutcracker*, *Swan Lake*, along with a few modern works. In a sense, it was a retrogressive step, for, unlike in Berlin, I did not get to dance many new works. However, the company was enormously appreciative of what I was doing, and I loved the ballerinas – Elaine Bauer and Marie Christine Mouis – I was working with. I also got more dancing than I would have if I had just remained with the National, and at this point, that was very important to me. From the first performance of *Giselle*, with Elaine Bauer, I was able to fit right in. Audiences and critics alike seemed happy.

In June 1985, our first child, Kyra, was born. I was present at the birth, there to see our little girl emerge quietly, with her eyes wide open. Our doctor commented that this was unusual. "She must have an old soul," he said. Erene had returned to her hospital room when I went to take a last look at Kyra before leaving the hospital and heading off home. She was held in an observation area, all neatly wrapped up in a little bundle. I stood there staring at her for a while, then turned away from the curtain, held my arm held against the hospital wall, and cried. I had hoped so much that everything would turn out well, and it had. We had a beautiful baby daughter. It was about five in the morning on a clear, crisp early-summer morning when I walked out of the hospital. Erene came home a few days later, with Kyra. After her four-month maternity leave, she decided she liked being at home with the baby. She resigned from her job.

Becoming a father and settling into a more domestic routine was not the only big change in my life. It was about this time that I made a conscious effort to revise the way in which I was training. Over the years, I had been plagued by a series of injuries, some minor, others not so minor. It began when I was eighteen, when I tore the lateral ligaments in my ankle. Now, I was thirty-two; injuries, plus the fear of them, were beginning to hamper my ability to function. I visited the Fitness Institute, and in a series of conversations with Len Quinn, the director, and physiotherapist Susan Shaw, we worked out a training program designed to prevent the injuries recurring. They first did an analysis of my body, then they gave me a combination of weight and aerobic training. The exercises were designed to strengthen my back and knees, putting equal emphasis on strength and speed.

With this new program, my days would begin not with company class, but with a workout at the Institute. I would then come into the studio and do my own class before going to rehearsal. The regime worked. For the first time in a long while, I wasn't taking Aspirin. I took Erik out to the Institute to show him the facilities and my program. Although he expressed interest, he did not pick up on my suggestion that it would be good to have a program like this, including physiotherapists, within the National. What I was doing was not generally understood in the ballet world at that time. It was considered eccentric. I felt then, and I feel now, that it is very old-school to say, If you don't do company class every day, you can't dance. Sometimes you need to do class on your own, and to do just what is right for your own body. The same thing is not always good for all the people all the time.

Karen complained about my not going to class. Although I tried to explain what I was doing, I don't think she ever really accepted or understood it. All she knew was that I was not there. I was not working hard alongside her any more. What had begun as a shared, enjoyable experience, and something quite special, had now turned sour. Now, when we worked together, she was highly critical of me. I'm still confused about it; I knew things were going wrong, but I did not understand why. What I saw as a better way to train, Karen — and I think Erik, too — saw as an excuse not to work. That made me feel guilty. I was convinced that Karen was disappointed in me, and not a little angry, too. At the back of my mind, I had always had the feeling that she considered herself a better dancer — something that went right back to the Moscow competition, where she won a medal and I didn't. She may never actually have felt this, but I believed that she did, and that was what counted. We both moved on, dancing together occasionally, but no longer on a regular basis. We were both travelling, and working outside Toronto, and it no longer seemed as important to be dancing together as it once had been. The years of the Gold Dust Twins were over.

At the same time, my relationship with Erik was deteriorating. I knew that he could be bitingly critical of other male dancers – there was always an edge here with Erik. For one thing, his standards were so high. How could they not be, when his own dancing was so glorious? Also, he had never, I think, quite reconciled himself to not dancing, which made those of us who were still dancing objects of both his criticism and his envy. That can be very uncomfortable. In many ways, Erik and I were not a good match. I needed a sense of approval from those for whom I was dancing, while Erik was always reluctant to give that unequivocal and unambiguous vote of confidence. One incident in particular now stands out in my mind as the cause of a major rift between us.

Carla Fracci, one of Erik's favourite partners, was to dance *Romeo and Juliet* with me at the O'Keefe Centre in April 1985. Joanne Nisbet and David Scott were taking the rehearsals, and, from the beginning, they did not go well. Carla was then close to fifty, well past her prime dancing years, and part of my role as her partner was to help her do the things that had once been much easier for her. I would move her into position in arabesque and do all the work in lifting, with little help from her. She even wanted me to partner her on a simple single turn. I desperately wanted to be helpful and accommodating, as I was well aware of her close relationship with Erik, but after a few very long rehearsals, there had been so much pressure on my lower back that the disc was inflamed. I had difficulty moving, let alone dancing. I couldn't bend. I phoned Erik and said I could not come in. I had been to the doctor, who told me to rest, saying that, if I didn't, I could do more damage. Erik asked me to at least come to the theatre. "I can't dance," I said. "You see the way she treats me, you see the work I'm doing. She's not helping me at all." Erik still pleaded for me to come in, at which point I lost it. I demanded to know whether or not he wanted me in the company. "I want to know right now," I added. "Frank, let's wait and talk when you are better," he said. He wanted me to dance, but I stood my ground. I would not dance with Carla. There was no one else in the company who could fill in, so at the last minute another dancer was brought in from Sweden. I don't think that Erik ever forgave me for this. I don't think he saw the injury as real at all. I think he thought he was honouring me by casting me with Carla. When the rehearsals turned out to be so brutal, I saw it as a form of abuse.

A far more serious injury, one that would sideline me for more than a year, occurred a few months later in Boston. This was pure accident, one of those awful chance things that you look back on and say, if only I had been one inch to the right, or if only I'd been a second later, it would not have happened. During a dress rehearsal of *Le Corsair*, which I was dancing with Marie Christine Mouis, I slipped on some droplets of oil that had been left on the stage. About to go into a grand jeté, I took off from the wrong position. There was so much pressure on the patella (kneecap) that the quads pulled it up, and the tendon was ripped from it, and the patella bone ended up halfway up my thigh. I still went up into the jump, but came down flat on my back. I was in shock, though, oddly, not in pain. "Will someone please bring the curtain down?" I asked.

Erene watched it all from the theatre balcony, holding Kyra, who was eight months old that day. She ran down to the stage, terrified. She had always had a fear in her when she watched me dance, a fear that something dreadful would happen. Now it had happened right before her eyes. She thought it was my back; everyone watching did. She cut me out of my harem-pants costume and helped me into my jeans. We then waited for the ambulance to come, which, in typical Boston traffic, seemed to take an eternity. At the hospital, they told me that, ironically, one of the best surgeons for the necessary operation was in Toronto. I flew back to Toronto a few days later, and the operation was performed by Dr. Robert Jackson at the Orthopaedic and Arthritic Hospital on

With Marie Christine Mouis, in rehearsal, just before my knee accident.

Wellesley. It involved reinforcing the patella tendon with Dacron, and I was told that, once it had healed, the break would never happen again. Dacron, it seems, unlike mere human tissue, doesn't break.

This was a highly unusual injury for a dancer — the doctors told me that they saw it most in power weightlifters and basketball players. That was small comfort. I was now thirty-three years old, and did not know how much longer I would be able to go on. The doctors had said there was no reason I should not return to dancing, but I could not escape the fact that I was getting older, and healing was taking longer. I was off for fourteen months, my longest period away from the stage, and, when I came back, I resigned from Boston, to work with the National. Once the shock wore off, Erene and I realized that neither of us had a paycheque. This really worried her until she found out that my lawyer, Michael Levine, had anticipated such an injury, and my contract gave me a year of disability on full salary. The day we arrived back in Toronto, Erene got two job offers. She decided to take on the launch of Cher's new fragrance, Uninhibited, in the Canadian market. I stayed home and looked after Kyra.

It was while I was away from the company that I got the news of Erik Bruhn's death. It came as a shock to me, as it did to everyone. He had gone into hospital, but it had not occurred to most of us that his illness was serious. A month later, he was dead. We had never been close. I had always been slightly uncomfortable around him, unsure of where I stood with him, wanting him to like what I did, while at the same time suspecting that he did not like it at all. None of this mattered now. All I could see was that the man who had reinvigorated the company, one of the greatest dancers of our time, a man for whom I had enormous admiration, was gone. When I returned to the company in April 1987, it was to a changed place, a place once again adrift.

~

Erik's death had left a gaping hole. Shortly before he died, he had passed down the "Ten Commandments" on how he would like the company to be run for the next few years. His three assistants, Valerie Wilder, Lynn Wallis, and choreographer Constantin Patsalas, were left to put these into effect. They struggled to do what Erik wanted, but on my return, I saw a group of very unhappy dancers. Constantin had disputed his position with the company, feeling that Erik wanted him to take on the role of artistic director. Valerie and Lynn didn't see it that way, and the company was embroiled in a bitter battle over both Constantin's role and the ownership of his choreography. Constantin himself had departed in November 1986, leaving the lawyers to sort things out. A general feeling of insecurity had settled in, particularly among the younger dancers. While Erik was alive, he had favoured them, giving them many opportunities to work under a guiding hand that they trusted implicitly. Now, no one knew who was making the decisions or what was going to happen next.

Although Constantin was in name still the company choreographer, the status of his works was in limbo. If he was the choreographer, and he was absent, where would the new work come from? Lynn Wallis, the second member of the triumvirate, taught a good class, supervised rehearsals well, and generally was a good representative of the company, but she did not have artistic vision. Valerie Wilder ran the business end very efficiently, but, like Lynn, she was not an artist. Through all of this, the board had taken no steps towards finding a replacement for Erik. A year passed, then another year, and still no search. Frustration among the dancers mounted – everyone was feeling the lack of artistic input and guidance. We were well coached, but I felt we were no longer going forward.

There was so much anxiety in the company that we held dancers' meetings, where everyone got to say what they thought was wrong. The complaints came thick and fast, about absolutely everything – from small things like rehearsal hours and casting, to the larger questions of lack of overall direction. The main question from everyone was: When are we going to get a new artistic director? Valerie didn't want to talk to us, Lynn was upset about it all, and Constantin wasn't there. Karen and Veronica, who were the dancers' representatives to the board, were among the most vocal about the problems. They talked to the board, but neither of them believed that they were being heard.

A collection of letters from dancers, in support of the position they had articulated, resulted in a meeting between Judy Cohen, the in-coming chairwoman, and the dancers. At this meeting, the dancers spoke out. We were rudderless, we said. In all of this, we were clear that there was not so much a problem with Erik's team as there was a problem with Erik's team without Erik. Erik had been the driving force, the linchpin. With him gone, the company was like a broken wheel. In the end, the board listened to us, and a serious search for a new artistic director was set in motion.

In the meantime, for me, it was back to dancing. My first performance in Toronto after my return was in April 1987, in *The Sleeping Beauty*, partnering one of the company's new ballerinas, Kimberly Glasco. Dancing with Kimberly was a delight – she was so easy to partner, always on her own balance. I had absolutely no worries with her, even though it was her first performance in a role that is technically one of the most demanding in the whole classical repertoire. Kimberly is a very cool lady. On this night, she had her nerves under control and seemed unfazed by the horrors of the Rose Adagio. All I had to do was keep my own nerves under similar tight rein, and get through it carefully. The doctor had said to me that there was no way this particular injury was ever going to happen again – not on that leg anyway. After all, I now had a Dacron patella tendon, which I had been assured would never rupture. Naturally, that didn't stop me worrying and being ultra-careful, but I hoped that artistry would cover this up. Thankfully, Rudolf had choreographed the Prince's role in such a way that you warmed up gradually as the ballet progressed. The choreography is a slow, two-hour preparation for the last solo, which is a real back-breaker. I got through it without any glitches, and woke the next day to find the reviews had only nice things to say about my return (which made me feel triumphant) – and even nicer things to say about Kimberly's debut.

I was back at work, and happy. I was made doubly happy that April, with the birth of our second child, Nicholas. It was only by lucky chance that I got to attend this birth. Erene was eight months' pregnant, and, knowing my travel schedule, was hoping the baby would be a bit premature. That didn't happen, so I had set out for Boston for a series of make-up performances, knowing that I would be away for a month, and that I would probably miss the birth. Luckily, my papers were not in order, and I was turned back at the border by American immigration. The following day, we went together to Erene's scheduled doctor's appointment. "I'm going to have the baby today," she told the doctor, who asked how she could be so sure. Somehow, she just knew. After the examination, we rushed straight to the hospital, and, after forty-five minutes of labour, voilà, Nicholas was born, arriving in the world with a worried look on his face. I had thought I wouldn't care if it were a girl or a boy, but now that we had a girl and a boy, my first thought was, "This is perfect. We've got one of each." The doctor brought me back to the real world and asked me if I wanted to cut the umbilical cord, handing me what looked like a pair of garden clippers. "It'll feel like cutting calamari," he said, which it did. I will be eternally grateful to the over-officious American immigration department for not letting me cross the border on that April morning, so I could be there for Nicholas Augustyn's debut onto the world stage.

Later that day, I called my father to give him the news. "Now you will not be alone," was his only comment. I wasn't quite sure what he meant by that. Did he mean I had a son who would carry on the family name? Or that a boy, unlike a girl, would be a buddy, a pal for the rest of my life? Or that a boy would be someone who would take care of me in my old age — hardly something you could expect a mere girl to do? Whatever he meant, he was glad I now had a boy. So was I.

Now, even though I was back at work, I knew that my time as a dancer was limited. I was thirty-four years old. Forty was then the upper limit for most male dancers, but I did not expect to be able to dance in the classics for that much longer. Throughout my career, I had been unusually plagued by injury. I had taken a total of two and a half years off from the stage, and that time didn't include the weeks off here and there due to more minor injuries. What I now wanted was to make sure that I quit before making an embarrassing spectacle of myself, as I had sadly watched Rudolf do towards the end of his career. How long I could go on I did not know, but gradually, when I felt I could no longer do justice to them, I began to say goodbye to roles that had been a fixture in my life for a very long time. There was no fanfare here, no farewell performance, just a quiet relinquishing amidst a sense of sadness and loss. In fact, I felt the loss of roles far more deeply than I would later feel my departure from the company. These roles were my friends; I had performed them so often, they had become a part of my being. You work so hard to develop a role. Then, by the time you really understand it, and have the skill to make it more powerful, your physical ability to perform it wanes. Although I had struggled with the character of the Prince in *Swan Lake*, it still saddened me to make the decision never to dance it again. It saddened me to give up the classical roles: in *Giselle*, *The Nutcracker*, and *Coppélia* — each had a place and meaning in my life; they were all defining rites of passage as a dancer. In this process of winding down, I first danced the roles less frequently, then gave them up altogether. My last two years with the National Ballet were spent almost exclusively in neo-classical and contemporary roles. Only rarely did I dance these with

Karen. My partners now included many of the younger ballerinas —
Kimberly Glasco, Sabina Allemann, and Kim Lightheart among them.
The works I was dancing still included a few classical warhorses, such
as *Don Quixote* and *La Bayadère*, along with the modern *Forgotten Land*,
and Kenneth MacMillan's *Song of the Earth*, a work of which I have
absolutely no memory, but which surviving photographs and the
schedule tell me I danced.

A highlight of these years was working with Glen Tetley on his
ballet *La Ronde*. Glen replaced Constantin Patsalas as the company's
artistic advisor in 1987. He had already given the company a wonderful ballet with *Alice*, his version of *Alice in Wonderland*. This was done
while I was away with the injury, and I never performed in it. *La Ronde*,
however, was done shortly after my return, and I was delighted to be
working with Glen again. His ballet *Sphinx* had been a favourite of
mine, so I was looking forward to the challenges Glen had for us.
Based on the play by Arthur Schnitzler, *La Ronde* is a series of pas de
deux, beginning with the Count and a Prostitute, who was memorably
danced by corps member Ronda Nychka, and moving through a series
of changing partners to end again, as the title suggests, with the
Prostitute. It is a highly compressed work, with the characters boldly
sketched in movement and costume, and for me, it is the quality of
Glen's choreography that lifts it beyond caricature. Glen's choreography is the most earthy, organic choreography I have ever danced. You
work his choreography, you don't float through it. It is a feeling almost
like kneading dough: you work it hard, turning it over. It's very
exhausting. As the Count, I had two pas de deux to dance, one with
Karen and one with Ronda.

For the first time, I was dancing the role of an older man, dressed
in street clothes, my hair greyed at the temples. That much was fine,
but Glen also gave the character some extremely physical choreography, of a kind that you would hardly expect an older character to be
able to perform. We had first tried some shuffling movements; Glen

With Karen, in La Ronde.

would shuffle along, and I would shuffle behind him, trying things out and reducing Karen, who stood watching, to gales of laughter. If it was that funny, it clearly didn't work, and another approach to age was needed. We settled on trying to capture a weightiness in the movement. Glen wanted a sense of authority, and that seemed the best way to try to get it across. What complicated things a little was that this character was also lecherous, and had to be playful with the women he was with. I don't know how successful I was in making the Count come alive, but it was a pleasure to watch Glen work, and see him get his inspiration from the dancers. No one inspired him more than Ronda, who was just seventeen, like a young colt, and incredibly versatile. Glen lit up when he watched her, and it inspired his choreography for all of us.

We took *La Ronde* to New York in 1988, along with *Onegin* and *Blue Snake*. I felt the season was something of a triumph for me, and, although I didn't know it at the time, it was to be the last time I danced in the city. I treasure the fact that Anna Kisselgoff, the *New York Times* dance critic, felt that the performance Sabina Allemann and I gave of *Onegin* on the second night outstripped that of the opening-night cast of imported stars, Natalia Makarova and Ivan Liska. We gave, Kisselgoff said, the "performance of a lifetime." Certainly the audience responded loudly, giving us a standing ovation. I felt that I had at last managed to get on top of the character of Onegin.

Maturity is a double-edged word for a dancer — it signals experience and understanding, but it can also be a euphemism for "no longer young" or, worse, "almost past it." The maturity that gave me the ability to cope with Onegin, and made it one of my favourite roles to dance, also meant that I would soon no longer be able, physically, to perform the role. That, sadly, is the tragedy of a dancer's life. It is not just a question of looks. Physically, you simply can no longer do it.

There was another kind of maturity that had led to a shift in the centre of gravity of my life. Having a young family changed things for me. I was no longer the carefree bachelor whose art was the only thing that mattered to him. Dancing was still vitally important to me, but that last injury had been something of a wake-up call. It signalled clearly to me that I wouldn't always be able to make a living this way. I needed to find a line of work where my ability to work didn't depend on the health of my body. Erene was working again so we would not be starving if I didn't work. Still, old ways of thinking die hard, and I was enough my father's son to feel that I should be the breadwinner. I started to look around at what other dancers did when they no longer danced.

If you wanted to stay in the dance world, the options were limited: you could teach, choreograph, or work in artistic administration. I had never really felt an interest in or shown an aptitude for choreography, and, while I enjoyed teaching on a part-time basis, I had never seen myself as a full-time teacher. What appealed most was the idea of running a company. I began to look around for a small company to work with.

During the winter of 1988–89, I heard that the Theatre Ballet of Canada, a company based in Ottawa, was looking for a new artistic director. It was a small group of about twelve dancers, and I thought this would be the perfect opportunity to make the break from full-time dancing. I did not want to stop dancing entirely and, when I talked to the Theatre Ballet board, they were happy with the idea that I continue to dance, along with taking on the job of running the company. I continued to work out my season with the National, doing a final round of performances of *La Ronde* on a tour of Germany in the summer of 1989. Then, without fanfare, at the end of July 1989, I quietly left the National Ballet of Canada, my theatrical home for eighteen years. Any sadness I might have felt was quickly submerged in the excitement of something new.

CHAPTER

I 4

Ottawa Ballet

I did not know what I was getting into when I took on the Theatre Ballet of Canada – and that was just as well. If I had known, I would not have done so, and that would have been a pity, for I would have missed out on some of the most intense and involving experiences of my life. During the five years I headed the company as its artistic director, Murphy's famous law was in full evidence: what could go wrong, did go wrong. For all those five years, my family barely saw me, and, when they did see me, they complained that all I ever talked about, lived, breathed, dreamed, was Theatre Ballet. There was always some crisis or other that needed to be managed, and it all came back to the same underlying problem, the usual one for small companies – lack of money.

The financial lifeblood of the small company is money from the Canada Council, which gives out operating grants based on assessors'

Stephanie Hutchison, now with the National Ballet, rehearsing in the Ottawa Ballet studios.

reports on the quality of the company and its work. The Council likes to see companies with a unique and innovative style. Often, these companies have been built around the work of a single choreographer, which was the case with the Theatre Ballet of Canada: since its beginning, it had been built around the work of its founder Larry Gradus. Larry's choreography was marked by its theatricality, since Larry was a man of the theatre as much as anything. A New Yorker at heart, he had struggled in Ottawa for several years, but by 1989, he had had enough. When I heard that the job was open, I called him. I didn't know Larry well, but had guested with his company, and knew and liked his work. Larry soon put a damper on my enthusiasm by giving me every reason in the world why I shouldn't take the job: there was no audience support in Ottawa for contemporary ballet, the Canada Council didn't like the company, the company's board was useless. He told me in no uncertain terms that it was a losing situation, and that "the gang" would kill me. Just who "the gang" were, I wasn't too sure, but it was no secret that there were disagreements between Larry and Celia Franca, who was now living in Ottawa and had, for a brief time, sat on the Theatre Ballet board. Larry resigned, and I enthusiastically, naïvely, insanely, took on the job he so clearly warned me not to take.

He wasn't the only one telling me not to take it. Erene wasn't keen about moving the family into an uncertain situation. Also, she had a good job working for a cosmetics and fragrance distributor, managing six national lines. However, it was work she could do equally well from Ottawa, so in the end she reluctantly agreed to the move. In July 1989 we packed up our High Park house and set off for the Glebe, our new neighbourhood in Ottawa. I drove down with our cat Mossy and the plants; Erene followed the next day, flying in with the children.

My first day on the job was a rude awakening. I was greeted by Gordon Pearson, the company's general manager, who, it turned out, was then the sole employee. He showed me around the empty offices and the two empty studios. "Where are the dancers?" I asked. I had made a lot of assumptions when I took the job on — basic ones, like there would be dancers on contract, and a repertoire for them to dance. Wrong, on both counts. The dancers had not had their contracts renewed, and Larry Gradus, who owned most of the company's repertoire, had withdrawn it. Larry, in all his warnings, had neglected to bring up this not-so-little point. Things got worse. The next day, I found out that there was no money (almost). The Canada Council had chosen the moment of my arrival to reduce the amount of the company's grant by a third. I pleaded with them to give me a chance. I'd just got there, I argued, I hadn't done anything that deserved punishment (at least, not yet). I begged them not to put me at a disadvantage for whatever they saw as Larry Gradus's shortcomings. But no amount of begging for a reinstatement of the grant at the previous year's level availed. Theatre Ballet was cut. It wasn't personal, they said — which naturally didn't stop me taking it very personally indeed.

To add to my woes, I found we were booked on an American tour, which was due to start in six weeks. I had to move, and move fast. The first thing I did was call the dancers in and rehire them. They were a motley crew, trained in different styles and of all shapes and sizes. Some of them could dance, some of them could dance, kinda, some of them not so well, some of them — well, they hadn't started dancing until their twenties. In truth, they were a ragged bunch and, as usual, the women were better than the men. Larry had clearly chosen them for personality as much as for dancing talent; I had just come from a big company, where there was a uniform look to the corps de ballet and personality was not something to be encouraged. Soloists were allowed to stand out a little, as were the kings and queens at the top, the principals. It was a rigid, heavy structure, demanding a definite look. Here, in Ottawa, there was no structure, no look. Just individuals, with their own strengths and weaknesses, who definitely did not come out of a cookie-cutter mould.

With dancers hired back on, I called Larry and persuaded him to let us dance a few of his works for the American tour, which somehow we managed to get through without incident. That over, I settled in to the daily problems of running a small company, while at the same time trying to work out a game plan for the long term. It was clear that the Canada Council could not be relied on for support – one way or another Theatre Ballet of Canada did not seem to fit easily within their mandate. So, if we were to survive, I had to look elsewhere for funding. That meant two sources: more from box-office revenues, and more from commercial or civic sponsorship. I spent an enormous amount of time and energy on the business of raising funds, far more than I should have done in an ideal world. No funds meant no company, so it had to be the first problem tackled. That meant that energy which should have gone into other things – like developing repertoire and searching out new choreographers – got less attention than it deserved.

I hadn't done much in the way of fundraising before. The closest I'd got to it was an association with Gala des Étoiles, which had been produced by Victor Melnikoff in Montreal to raise funds for the children's hospitals in the Montreal area. Since 1985, I had worked with Victor on this, both appearing in the gala as a performer and acting as its artistic director. This aside, fundraising was new to me, and I didn't know the do's and don'ts, which was just as well, because there was no "it can't be done" hanging around in my head to hold me back. If I had an idea, I just went ahead and did it. You couldn't dignify what I did by calling it a strategy – it was more a piecemeal effort, improvising as I went along, taking advantage of every opportunity and trying to create them where they didn't exist.

Early on, we decided to have a gala to raise funds. I wanted the company to present a new work at the gala, and thought that Francis

Patrelle's *Come Rain, Come Shine* would be a perfect gala piece. Set to songs made famous by Judy Garland, it is a series of duets danced within the confines of a boxing ring. Essentially a crowd pleaser, I thought it would be an entertaining draw. But it was going to cost forty thousand dollars, and the board said no. It was too expensive.

"Whatever happened to the two-thousand-dollar ballets we used to do?" one member asked. "Larry used to create ballets that only cost two thousand dollars."

"You weren't paying the choreographer," I replied, "and there were hardly any costumes. We're moving on, we're not doing two-thousand-dollar ballets any more." I argued the case, but they were adamant.

I left the board meeting and went straight to the phone, called the president of Cartier, and gave him my idea for the ballet. "Sounds good," he said. "Send me some material." I did this, and he called back to say he liked it. In return for a few promotional items, he signed on. "Merry Christmas," he said. "You've got forty thousand dollars. I'll get a cheque out to you tomorrow." I remember the date, December 23. It was one of the best Christmas presents I ever had in my life. I had come from a company where hundreds of thousands of dollars were spent on a single ballet, and here they had been wondering what happened to the two-thousand-dollar ballets. We had to think bigger than that. I felt forty thousand dollars was not an outrageous amount for a new ballet by a company with a total budget of around one million. Now, with the money in the bank, I was able to go ahead. The gala was a great success — Karen came and danced with me in *Come Rain, Come Shine* — and at the end of the day we cleared forty-five thousand dollars and had a new ballet in the repertoire.

What helped us keep afloat as a company ironically helped dig our grave with the Canada Council. The Council sends out its assessors to monitor the progress (or otherwise) of the companies it funds. They had taken a "wait and see" approach to the company when I first took over, but their thoughts on *Come Rain, Come Shine* were uniformly negative. I never did know who the assessors were — their reports, in a recent change of policy, were now anonymous, partly to protect them from angry assessees, such as the Montreal choreographer who was rumoured to have thrown bricks through their windows when he didn't like what they had to say about him. Given what they had to say about us, I might have been tempted, so perhaps it's just as well I didn't know who they were. "There's all the difference in the world between this stuff (which is all very well as marketing) and what a dance company should seriously be doing, which is putting its best effort into making art," one wrote. Another commented that they were "enraged to see such a large Ottawa audience giving a warm reception to this kind of ballet. Are they dazzled by Frank Augustyn's pirouettes or suave appearance — is that what they like, is that what they want, is that what they should get? That kind of company will keep dance and especially ballet in a nauseating rot." Well, that was embarrassingly blunt, but it did set me thinking. The Canada Council had at least one assessor who was enraged because the audience liked us. For us to survive, I had to make sure the audience did like us, which did not augur well for how we sat with the Canada Council.

What I wanted to do in Ottawa was build a company based on classical training, while creating an environment where they could dance not just classical works but also neo-classical and contemporary pieces. I was looking for an eclectic balance, without specializing in any one thing. We'd do the odd pas de deux from the classics, things we could handle, along with neo-classical and contemporary work from a variety of choreographers. I wanted to bring in new creations, but also some older established works. I had in mind Fleming Flindt's *The Lesson* and José Limón's *The Moor's Pavane*. I also wanted to work with Canadian choreographers, and search for choreographic talent within the company. Setting about doing this, that first year, I was exhilarated, planning, forecasting, fundraising, and dreaming a little.

One of the first things I thought we needed was a Christmas show. We were far too small to attempt something like *The Nutcracker*, so I thought that Hans Christian Andersen's fairytale *The Tin Soldier* might work for us. Timothy Spain choreographed the piece for us, with Robert Swerdlow composing the score, and Mary Kerr designing sets and costumes. The production used all our twelve dancers, along with three children and some stand-ins. The board was impressed with the idea; they were less impressed with the cost, which in the end amounted to $350,000. I also had serious worries about how we were going to pay for it.

More out of desperation than anything else we started a "build a ballet – buy a costume" scheme. Erene began the process by asking designer Oscar de la Renta if he would buy a couple of costumes. He bought the Tin Soldier and Paper Ballerina costumes, and we publicized this to get the scheme started. A Frog costume cost fifteen hundred dollars, a child's costume cost six hundred dollars. You could even buy the props and sets if you wanted to: the whole production was up for sale. This went a short way towards defraying the costs, and it had the added benefit of guaranteeing an interested audience.

Our first performance of *The Tin Soldier* was in December 1990 at the National Arts Centre theatre, with Stephanie Hutchison as the Paper Ballerina. I danced the title part. We sold out, and for the two following years we mounted the production in the Opera, eventually paying back the costs of the production and making money on it. Aimed at seven-year-olds, I can't say that *The Tin Soldier* was high art – but then, neither is *The Nutcracker*. Once again, it was a case of the audience loving us, and the Canada Council being somewhat less than keen. "A standing ovation no less!!! I am afraid I could not bring myself to join in," was one comment. "One might have thought this was the premier of some great new classic judging by the response." Another noted that the choreography was a failure at every level, while the music was an undistinguished hodgepodge and the dancers mediocre. "The opening-night audience was properly psyched and gave the company a standing ovation," another wrote in disbelief. Well, I thought, you can't please all of the people all of the time. That was, to put it mildly, unfortunate. We needed to please them all if we were to survive in a world where funding came from a combination of box-office and sponsorship revenues, and granting agencies. It might have been very different if the Canada Council had been the sole source of our funding. Or if — impossible thought — we had some commercial fairy godfather or -mother who would totally finance us. Either would have allowed us to go in a single direction, without concern for audience. As it was, whatever schizophrenic solution we came up with in the complex mix of funding that was our reality was almost certainly doomed to fail. That it took as long as it did was in no small measure due to my stubbornness. I was not going to give up easily, even if the critics thought what I was doing was an artistic disaster — which, from what they were writing, seemed to be the case.

It was during our time in Ottawa that Erene decided to change careers. For a long time, she had wanted to do something that had more human meaning than marketing cosmetics. Her background was in psychology, and she had been thinking of going back to school to qualify as a teacher. One incident gave her the impetus she needed. While travelling for Oscar de la Renta Fragrances, she had a breakfast meeting with the president. "I'm glad to hear that Kyra's okay," he said. She was shocked. She hadn't even known there was a problem — I hadn't told her, as I didn't want to worry her — but Kyra had a temperature of 104 degrees, and I had taken her to the hospital. That was it for Erene. She quit her job, returned to school, got her B.Ed., specializing in special education, and embarked on a new career as a teacher of children with learning disabilities. This had the added benefit of giving her more time at home with Kyra and Nicholas, which was what she wanted. It was just as well, because I was hardly there. My family was resigned to seeing me only occasionally. Work was a total preoccupation, to the exclusion of almost everything else – even how I looked. One day, I was waiting for Erene, Kyra, and Nicolas at the bus stop, outside the liquor store. A man came out of the liquor store, and, seeing me, dug into his pocket. Much to my surprise, he offered me some coins. "Here ya go, buddy," he said. I turned around to face myself in the window. Reflected back was a normally clad dancer: white Nikes, casual, loose-fitting khakis, a red and yellow plaid shirt, and, because I had taken a shower after a dancing day, wet hair. I wanted to give my face a rest, so I hadn't shaved. Dancer or rubby? Who could tell? In that instant, I remembered my father. Every day, after finishing work at Stelco, he would shower, shave, and put on a plain, crisp shirt, pressed pants, and black, polished shoes. I never actually saw him at work, but I had an image of him there – molten steel dripping from his helmet, metallic dust covering his protective clothing and steel-toed workboots. He always said to me, people judge your character by the way you dress. Wear neat clothes, and be clean. He was a very proud man. Well, as I looked at myself in the liquor-store window, at least I could say that I was clean. I can well imagine what my father would have said to me. The next morning, I went to work wearing a suit and tie. I had a meeting with a potential sponsor. With any luck, I thought, the suit and tie would bring in more than just a few coins.

After a year and a half in Ottawa, I had changed the name of Theatre Ballet of Canada to Ottawa Ballet, to affirm the company's roots in the community. By now, I was beginning to get the picture with the Canada Council: the more commercial we were, the more we appealed to a popular audience, the less they seemed to like us. Why could they not accept us as a regional ballet company? There are many such companies in the United States, and their mandate is, for the most part, an eclectic one, although there are exceptions, such as the Miami Ballet, run by Edward Villella, which is centred on the work of George Balanchine. Most of these mid-sized companies perform works in a wide range of styles. Why did the Council not see a need for such a company in Ottawa? They had an orchestra and an opera company, but no ballet company. We could serve the region, and at the same time tour in smaller venues that companies like Royal Winnipeg Ballet could not serve. Instead of accepting this, the Council had only one repeated question: What is your niche?

Although problems with funding meant that I spent less time in the studio than I should have, the time I had there was both demanding and invigorating. Working with the dancers was the single most enjoyable part of being with Ottawa Ballet, and it has left me with vivid memories of some remarkable people. They came from the four corners, and not all of them had the most perfect training or the most ideal bodies for classical dance. What they did have was desire, and in a small company that doesn't require the almost anorexic look that has now overtaken classical ballet, this counted for a lot. They also had character, which is not to say that this doesn't exist in larger companies, only that it so often has to be submerged in support of the form. At Ottawa Ballet, character was a definite plus.

There was Carlos Loyola, from South America, a man's man, whose life began after the curtain rang down. He would get dressed up, ready to go, his black hair moussed back and shiny, small tie, white shirt, nice jacket with a sheen, tight black pants, and the right boots – the boots were very important. Carlos was a knockout, and the women were falling all over him. He loved salsa, and, even on tour, he knew exactly where to go for it, sometimes getting the women from the company to go along with him. I went once too, and was amazed. Carlos was the star of the dance floor. This man should not be in ballet, I thought, after watching him salsa. He does this so much better. Rumba, tango, salsa — his salsa was absolutely incredible and his tango was pretty good, too. Carlos had star quality, and he brought that to the ballet stage. He did not have great technique, and he was always hurting, always in a lot of pain. But, if he was placed in the right ballet, with the right character, your eye would always go to him. He had a great, almost explosive, feeling, as if anything could happen. Carlos developed an audience, mostly women, who were always waiting for him at the stage door. Eventually, I had to talk to him about his late nights. He would come in in the mornings, looking terrible. "Carlos," I'd say, "you cannot come in again looking like this. You can't be having your first coffee five minutes before the rehearsal starts."

"Yes, yes, Frank. I know. I drink too much, I do too much salsa, too many women, women is my problem, I know, I know," he would say, with a kind of world-weary charm that told me that he wasn't ever going to change.

When I first saw Igor, I thought I had found a different kind of star. Igor came via a contact at Gala des Étoiles. He was tall, over six feet, and looked a little anaemic, but his Russian training was excellent. He could do everything — excellent jumps, good turns, equally good right and left. I was delighted he could work with us. Then, the first week he was with us, he got a really bad toothache. His face swelled up, and I assumed he had an abscess. The company had a dental plan — or rather, we had a board member whose husband was a dentist. As a result we got not cheap dental work (I had learned a thing or two about PR by now) but high-quality, inexpensive dental work. Igor was in terrible shape, so I took him to the high-quality, inexpensive dentist, and left him there. The dentist called me to say that, if he didn't do something, Igor would lose all his teeth. "This guy can dance," I said. "I need him. Do what you have to." So the dentist proceeded to work on Igor. Day after day. Igor would come into the studio groaning, in constant pain. Eventually, the dentist called to say the treatments were over. The next day, Igor was gone. Disappeared. I haven't seen him since. Three days before a tour, Igor, the sneak, disappeared. He had learned all the roles, got his teeth fixed, and gone. I phoned around, but couldn't find him. If I had, I would have been tempted to pull every tooth out myself — he had left me in the lurch and I had to rejig the whole program for the tour to work around his absence.

Marie-Claude Sabourin was a thorn in my side, and I loved her for it. She was always asking me questions. She'd never leave me alone. It was great, because I needed that questioning and I depended on her to do it. Whenever there was a plan — casting or schedule — there she was, questioning. If we had been a union company with a union rep, it would have been Marie-Claude. As a dancer, she had one of the most difficult bodies to work with — she wasn't very flexible, didn't have great arches in her feet, had a long trunk with shorter legs, yet, despite all these disadvantages, what she did on stage was very special. Marie-Claude gave one hundred per cent, and her talents shone through in interpretation.

Then there was the dancer I hired blind, who turned out at first to have absolutely no interpretative skills at all. Li Yaming, a Chinese dancer in the company, came to me one day, saying that he had a friend who wanted to get out of Beijing. He showed me his friend's photograph.

"Can he dance?" I asked.

"Much better than me," said Yaming. "And he's six foot tall."

"If he's better than you, and he's that tall, I'll bring him over," I said. I decided to take the risk, and went through the process of getting Yaming's friend, Ping Feng, into the country. Feng turned out to be an instinctive dancer. Boy, could he dance. He was one of the best dancers we ever had, but there was a problem. His technique was all there, but

he had absolutely no expression. He found it hard to get used to the
idea that no one would arrest him if he made a funny face on stage,
since he had come from a structured training regime where individual
expression was frowned on. I encouraged him to interpret. No one was
going to come and arrest him and take him back, I said, if he put a little
expression into things. He then went so far overboard that we had to
pull him back. In *Come Rain, Come Shine* Francis Patrelle was directing
him, telling him that, as he was wooing the girl, he had to be sexy. Feng
started dancing away and grabbing his crotch. Francis stood there,
staring in disbelief. "No, Feng," he said. "You have to be suggestive, not
blatant." Feng quickly developed into an extremely sensitive artist – to
the degree that you would have thought he had been brought up this
way. He wasn't. You had to be there at the beginning to appreciate what
he became. In five years, his interpretative skills grew in a manner that
it takes most dancers fifteen years to accomplish. I had enormous
respect for him, his talents, and the way he worked.

Feng was at the centre of one of the most delicate situations of
my time at Ottawa Ballet. I had brought in Edward Hillyer, from
Montreal, to choreograph for us. I was full of admiration for Edward.
I loved the way his choreography covered space – he made his dancers
really move across the stage. His work had a lot of life, which the
company very much needed. He was also infectiously positive. The
dancers wanted to be in that studio and working with Edward,
because of his positive way. Unfortunately, in the course of working
with the company, Edward became infatuated with Feng, and Feng, in
his naïve and friendly way, with his poor English, had led Edward to
believe he was in love with him. Feng's background had not exposed
him to homosexuality, which meant he was confused and a little disturbed by Edward's approaches – and reproaches. For a long time, he
didn't say anything about it, because he thought I would fire him, and
things festered. Finally, it got so bad that Feng showed up in my office

to talk about it. He explained that he was just trying to do what Edward wanted, he was trying to be friendly. He didn't want any trouble, he just wanted to work. He liked it here, he wanted to stay.

I was taken completely by surprise. I hadn't known anything was going on. I told Feng I would speak to Edward, which I did. For about an hour and a half. Edward was convinced that Feng loved him, but that he was pushing him away for one of the girls. "Then we should talk about it," I said. "There's nothing more to talk about," he said. Nonetheless, I kept talking to Edward, not just that day, but day after day, focussing him on his work. I reassured Feng that everything would work out fine. Eventually, the pressure of opening night took over – the ballet *Le Corps Constellé*, an abstract piece set to Dvořák's *Serenade for Strings*, was a great success, Feng danced in it beautifully, and Edward departed for home with his dream of Feng still intact.

When I had first walked into the company, I made it a policy that, if any dancer wanted to see me, day or night, I would take time away from what I was doing, because that was where my priority lay – with the dancers. Sometimes I got pulled out of board meetings to talk to dancers, but I never wanted dancers to feel that their needs were not listened to and taken care of, or that, as artistic director, I was distant from them. I had been on the short end with distant artistic directors, and I didn't want that to happen to any dancers working for me. It was made a little easier by the fact that I was still dancing with them, and taking daily class alongside them. I tried to bring in works that developed the strengths they had. Not all of them had everything, but what I was able to do with what they had, was amazing. It made me proud of them, and it made me feel good about myself, too. They worked so hard, and, at the end of the day, they gained so much and were so appreciative.

Continuing to train while running a company added to the length of my working day, to the point where it began to have a serious effect

Above: Ottawa Ballet, in Edward Hillyer's Le Corps Constellé.

Below: Ottawa Ballet, the company in the studio, 1993.

on my marriage. I was working seven days a week – and they were seven long days. I found it impossible to let go of the company, because there was always another crisis to solve. Eventually, Erene said to me that, even when I was physically at home, I wasn't really there. "Where am I in your life?" she asked. "Where are the kids in your life?" I had to admit that I was putting far more effort into the company than I was into my family. I knew that, if I didn't, the company would collapse. Then again, if the situation wasn't resolved soon, my marriage might be the thing that disintegrated.

Overriding everything was the constant struggle over money. Every year, for five years, the Canada Council cut our grant. Their assessors continued to write caustic reports on the quality of the company's repertoire and programming, although their comments about the dancers and the quality of the dancing improved. It seemed that, from their point of view, as an artistic director, I could not do anything right. I brought in popular works, and these were dismissed as trash. I brought in Balanchine – and he was dismissed as being beyond the dancers' capabilities. I brought in José Limón's classic *The Moor's Pavane*, and while this was generally appreciated – in performances danced by Karen, who guested with us, myself, Marie-Claude Sabourin, and René Daveluy – they suggested that the work could not have been done without Karen. Works from new choreographers were generally dismissed. Even Edward Hillyer's two pieces, *Le Corps Constelle* and *A Priori*, liked by most of the assessors, by the dancers, and by the audience, had their detractors who thought them uninventive. Nothing, however, brought more controversy than Fleming Flindt's 1963 work *The Lesson*, based on the Eugène Ionesco play.

On one level, this was a definite success. It was well danced, particularly by Marie-Claude Sabourin, Louis Martin Charest, and Tonia Stefiuk. Not surprisingly, given its creators, it was an intensely dramatic work. The story is that of a ballet master who, with the help of his assistant, murders a succession of female students. Judging by this bald plot description, it was not a work likely to appeal to any feminists in the audience. One of our board members, Sheilagh McGonigle, was also a member of the Women's Legal Education and Action Fund (LEAF), and she was outraged by it all, leaving the theatre with loud comments about how disgusting the whole thing was. I woke up the next day to find the Ottawa press had taken up the story. Sheilagh was vociferous in her criticism of the piece, arguing that it endorsed violence against women, and she promptly resigned from the board. "What are we teaching our children?" she asked. "That it's okay to be violent to women?" I was taken aback. No one, to my knowledge, had criticized this ballet in this way before. For more than thirty years, it had been considered one of the great pieces in the neo-classical repertoire. Always, as far as I knew, it had been read as an allegory: the dancing master represented Hitler, the students, the people of Germany, the pianist, the Gestapo. When first performed for television in Denmark in 1963, it had won the prestigious Prix Italia as the best TV program of the year. Times, it seemed, had changed since then. Allegories only work when the audience understands what is being allegorized, and to my horror, many of our audience were also taking the story literally. Maybe I should have understood this and not done the work – certainly, violence against women is not something that I would want to endorse. Although equally, it does exist, and *not* representing it doesn't mean that it will go away. Needless to say, all the controversy meant that the rest of our run with that program sold out. We could have sold another week, if we could have stayed in the theatre, which unfortunately for our box-office situation was already booked.

We did not always sell out in Ottawa, even though we struggled mightily to grow roots in the community. The name change had helped with our profile, and we did performances in the park every year, and community outreach programs where we performed in schools. But when all is said and done, Ottawa is just not a big enough place to support a company year round. As a result, for long stretches of time, we were on the road. This was a whole new experience of touring for me. No more New York and London, now we were on the road to places like Red Deer, Churchill Falls, Goose Bay, and Gander. In some ways, touring was easier than with the National. At least now we had more room on the bus, and it was easier to check into hotels when there were only about fifteen of us! That said, the hotels, while cheaper, definitely left something to be desired. One hotel in Kingston that promised thirty charming rooms did not live up to that promise. Yes, the rooms were nicely furnished in period style, decent and clean. Trouble was, the band that performed downstairs after hours vibrated the whole hotel: my lamp moved, the glasses rattled, and none of us could sleep.

Gander was a high point. For one thing, the presenter was delighted, we had almost completely sold out. As we counted on selling 35 per cent, and our fee was based on this, it meant we had made him a lot of money. After the performance, we went to the only place that was open, a pizza house. While we were there, some of the audience came in. They did something that would have been unheard of in a larger centre – they waited until we had finished eating, and then came over to ask for our autographs. It was one o'clock in the morning, and mothers and fathers were standing there, waiting patiently with their children. One young girl asked for my autograph, and gave me an envelope. "I've made you this," she said. In the envelope was a blue-and-white friendship bracelet, which she had braided. I was touched; I wore it for the rest of the tour. It was a small moment, but it reinforced what I was trying to do. I wanted to give these people quality work, understandable work, that they could enjoy. For most of my life I had been performing in the big centres – Toronto, Montreal, London, New York, San

Francisco. Yet now I was getting almost as much satisfaction bringing ballet to places from Red Deer to Goose Bay, places that otherwise might never get the chance to see a live performance. Nothing, for me, will ever quite beat the satisfaction of performing, but this came a very close second.

In the end, it all fell apart in a rather ugly way. In 1993, the Canada Council, citing our negative assessors reports, pulled the plug on the company. Without the Canada Council, it might have been possible to go on, if I had had the energy. But after five years of struggle, I was emotionally exhausted. Five years of keeping the company together, finding dancers, finding choreographers, acquiring new works, rehearsing the dancers, training to keep myself fit to dance – and always, always fundraising. By the fourth year, we even had a small surplus, and at that point, I had let the board know that I was going to move away from fundraising, to concentrate more on the dancers and the repertoire, which is where my energies should have been in the first place. I had spent far too much time at my desk on the phone. Unfortunately, without the constant attention, the money did not come in, and, in the end, there was only enough money to pay the company – not me. I finally quit after working for fifteen weeks without pay.

Ottawa Ballet was both an exciting and bruising experience. I still find it hard to talk about evenly, without anger in my voice. What I wanted was simple: to bring quality ballet, on a small and eclectic scale, to smaller communities. Right from the very beginning with the dramatic Canada Council cuts, I feel my efforts were compromised. The cuts forced me to take an ad hoc approach to fundraising, going in all directions to try to raise money. This I willingly did, but in retrospect, I am not at all sure that you can effectively serve the different masters of the Canada Council, the box office, and corporate sponsors. The Council wanted serious work that pushed the frontiers of the art form. The audience wanted to be entertained. Sponsors wanted something they could be proud of. Only rarely did these three desires coincide. It is hard to have clarity of vision in such circumstances, particularly amidst the turmoil of constant crisis. What happened at Ottawa Ballet, where I was trying to serve three very different masters with three very different tastes and agendas, is a small object lesson in what can go wrong when mixed funding provides mixed direction.

<hr/>

While I was in Ottawa I crossed paths with Rudolf Nureyev again. Over the years, we had kept in touch, although we now rarely saw each other. The last time I had danced with him had been at a gala for the National Ballet in 1987, in *Songs of a Wayfarer*. Rudolf had demanded that I dance with him, not in the role which I usually danced, which he was to take, but in the role of the alter ego. Tomas Schramek, who usually danced this part, spent many generous hours in the studio, teaching it to me. Ever the consummate professional, he did this with enthusiasm and without complaint – even though he was giving up a role for which he had received great acclaim.

Rudolf had arrived in Toronto only a day before the performance. Tomas supervised a late-night rehearsal for us, which was productive and pleasant, but it was clear that Rudolf was tired and preoccupied. There was none of the usual horsing around, no sexual innuendos, no clever remarks. He seemed to be in a "let's get it done" mode. Only later did the reason for this become clear. He had been diagnosed HIV-positive three years earlier and everything was now urgent for him. I did not know that at the time. None of us did.

Rudolf was pleased with the rehearsal and went off with his usual entourage for dinner. I stayed behind in the studio, working on the

With Rudolf, during a dress rehearsal of Songs of a Wayfarer.
The following night's performance was the last time we appeared on stage together.

steps. I was anxious, and spent a restless night. The next day, I arrived at the theatre early, went through my warm-up, and felt as prepared as I could be for the role. On stage, before the performance, I was trying out a few steps when the five-minute call was announced and Ernie, our stage manager, asked where Rudolf was. I didn't know, but went to check. Back in the dressing room, Rudolf was nowhere close to ready. He didn't even have his costume on. And he hadn't yet spray-painted his shoes. He asked me to do this for him, so I grabbed what I hoped was the right colour, and did a very nice job of painting my hands along with the shoes. At that moment Ernie came to the dressing-room door and stood there with a look of disbelief on his face, as he took in Rudolf, only half-dressed, and me with paint all over my hands. Ernie tapped his watch and held his hands as if in prayer. We bolted up onto the stage. As there were still a few seconds to spare, I thought I could get some of the still-wet paint off my hands with some Kleenex. It just made it worse. The Kleenex stuck to my hands, which now looked both painted and feathered. There was nothing to do but rub them furiously, which helped a bit. Then lights went to black, the curtain began to rise. Rudolf turned to me and wished me *merde*, the dancer's good-luck wish.

As the music started and the spotlights came up, I couldn't help thinking that what had just happened would make a perfect scenario for a nightmare, but I quickly brushed that thought aside, and put myself into performance mode, although it was a strangely conscious performance. I was not in command of the new role. It was so odd for me to watch Rudolf dance my part, the part that I felt had always been mine. It was almost as though I were watching myself. That should be me out there in the blue costume, the young, naïve soul. Rudolf should be where I was — dancing the all-knowing, all-seeing spirit of reality. That was more the way it had always been between us. For so many years, Rudolf had been an inspiration to me. His was the image of a male dancer that I had followed, learned from, even imitated for a while. Now, on this stage for one brief moment, it seemed the roles were reversed. I was the mature one, he was the one trying to recreate the innocence of youth. I felt I must not let him down. At the end of the performance, for the last time, I was able to enjoy being there with Rudolf, basking in the ovation given to us by the sold-out house, as Tomas stood beaming at us from the wings.

A few years later, Rudolf had given up classical dancing, and was touring in a production of *The King and I*. He came through Ottawa, and I invited him out for dinner after the performance with a group of friends, among them Celia Franca. It turned out to be an unpleasant evening; he got quickly drunk, and on his way back from a trip to the washroom, began pawing some of the other restaurant patrons. I had my back to him and didn't see this, but Celia Franca was watching. "Frank," she said, "I think you must take care of our friend."

I brought him back to the table, and, when it was time to leave, took him out to the limousine. I literally had to carry him, with his arm over my shoulder. I leaned him against the limo while I went to open the door, and, as I turned back to get him, I saw him approaching two very large, husky, leather-clad men. He went right up to them and started touching them. These were bikers, with beards, dark glasses, and tattoos, and they looked as if they might beat the living daylights out of us both. I grabbed Rudolf by the shoulders and literally threw him into the limousine, told the driver to take him back to his hotel, and slammed the door. The car took off with Rudolf sprawled across the back seat, leaving me to — so to speak — face the music. "How are you guys doing?" I greeted the bikers nervously, and, without waiting for an answer, hustled back into the restaurant, happy to make it in one piece. The next day I called Rudolf to make sure he was okay. He had no memory of what had happened, but the story made him laugh. "Were they good-looking?" he asked, adding with characteristic crudeness, "How big were their cocks?"

Two years later, he had transformed himself again – into a conductor. He had just conducted a performance of *Romeo and Juliet* at the Met in New York, which I had enjoyed. I called him in Paris and asked if he would conduct the National Arts Centre orchestra in a work I was choreographing for Ottawa Ballet, with music by Dvořák. He was a little worried about doing it with a full orchestra. "Musicians are afraid of it," he said. "Maybe we had better not do it." Musicians are frightened of it? He was frightened of it. We talked about it a bit, and he said he was now heading off to his place in St. Bart's in the Caribbean. He had just seen through the premier of his new production of *La Bayadère* for the Paris Opéra and was going to his island home to recuperate. He said I should call him there. He sounded tired. I knew there was something wrong with him, but I couldn't bear to believe the rumour that he had AIDS.

I called him a few days later in St. Bart's. "Why don't you come down and visit?" he asked. I said I didn't have the time, I had a company to run. "Come if you can," he said, "before it's too late." I put the phone down. Before it's too late? Maybe the rumours were true. I called my travel agent and went down the very next day. It was November, there were storms, the journey took me eighteen hours, but I finally made it.

What I saw when I arrived at the house was a waif of a man, lying on a bed in an alcove looking out onto the sea. I went and sat on the bed, and he glared at me, as if I had invaded his territory, but I wanted to be near him, to touch him and talk to him. All the time, his dog, Soloria, was pacing around. "This bitch is the only woman I have not been able to get into bed with me," he joked. I knew then his spirit was not entirely gone, but his body, his beautiful body, was wasted. I was suffused with sadness. He was, in so many ways, a noble man and this was not a noble end. We talked about Karen and Veronica and the National, about Erene and the children. We made plans for his trip to Ottawa, to conduct Beethoven's *Eroica* at our gala in March. It was business as usual, an affirmation of the future. There was no mention of sickness, no mention of death or dying. Yet I only had to look at him to know that he was not going to make it to Ottawa. I did not want to believe what I was seeing. I told myself, he has made recoveries before. He can do it again. He is the strongest man I know.

It was the last time I saw him. Two months later, he was dead.

C H A P T E R
—————————
1 5

Footnotes

W ith my departure from Ottawa Ballet, at forty-one years of age,
I was now in a situation dreaded by all aging dancers. I was unem-
ployed. I had reinvented myself once – the dancer had become an
artistic director. Now I was going to have to reinvent myself again.
The only world I knew was ballet, and I wanted to stay within it.
Other dancers have completely reinvented themselves, a prospect that
to me was both uninteresting and daunting. Wendy Reiser, a soloist
with the company, went back to school and became a doctor, Linda
Maybarduk turned to writing, Veronica Tennant has become an
accomplished television producer. Rex Harrington is talking about
landscaping when he retires. That's fine for them, but I had no real
interest in anything but dance. I had always known what I wanted to
do, and I had done it. So what now? All the dance companies in

—————————

My new role as host of Footnotes. *Kimberly Glasco, the show's ballerina, is behind me.*

Canada had artistic directors. The National had appointed James Kudelka, and there were no other immediate options.

Moses Znaimer, the tzar of Citytv, came to the rescue. He and his wife, Marilyn Lightstone, live in my Toronto neighbourhood, to which I had returned in 1995. One day, I was cycling past Moses' house and stopped off to say hello. Moses was just starting the Canadian version of Bravo!, the arts network. "Do some ballet programs for me," he suggested.

"Yes, but what?" I asked.

"How about the top ten?"

"The top ten what?"

"The top ten ballets," he replied, probably thinking, Is Frank stupid, or what? I decided it was a good idea, and set to work finding people to work with.

Neil Bregman of Sound Venture Productions in Ottawa had worked on *The Tin Soldier* with me, so I approached him with the idea. He liked it, and we set about working on a proposal, which we called *Footnotes*. My idea for the shows was to bring the world of ballet to the television audience in a fast and furious way. *Footnotes* was to be a combination of ballet history, extracts from great performances, and interviews with some of the most prominent dancers of our time, all melded together by me, the genial host and guide. It was very important to me that the shows be alternately light-hearted and serious, not an easy thing to pull off, but I think, in the end, we managed it. Above all, I wanted to demystify ballet and make it accessible to ordinary people, and to try to recreate for them, as well as for myself, the excitement I felt when I first saw that magical performance of *La Sylphide* as a young boy. We took it to Paul Gratton, then the commissioning editor at Bravo!, and he gave us the commission.

All we now had to do was raise the rest of the money and make the shows. Doing *Footnotes* was a lifeline for me. I was able to work and be with dancers. If I couldn't dance any more, I could talk to people about dancing, and in the process try to come to a greater understanding of what my working life to that point had been about.

Footnotes was a chance to develop a primer on ballet for a far larger audience than I had ever reached on stage. Directors Derek Diorio and Katherine Jeans, writers Dan Lalande and Michael Laewen, and I were all determined to make the shows accessible. That led us to an irreverent and often humorous approach. We mocked partnerships in a fake "marriage" ceremony, dropped ten-ton weights on a male dancer in sympathy with his lot of carrying the ballerina around, cut pointe shoes in half with a saw to show how thin they really were, and talked about dance belts, which prompted British dancer Anthony Dowell to observe that companies would probably sell far more tickets if men did not wear them.

Our first aim was to tell the stories of the most popular ballets – Moses' "top ten," which turned out to be a "top eight" – *Swan Lake*, *The Sleeping Beauty*, *La Sylphide*, *Coppélia*, *Giselle*, *Cinderella*, *Don Quixote*, and *Romeo and Juliet*. Then, we did shows on ballerinas, the male dancer, music, galas, and partnership. Finally, we did country reports on Diaghilev's Ballets Russes, and the history of ballet in Russia, France, England, China, and Canada. That was an awful lot to do on the minuscule budget we had for each show, but somehow we managed to put the half hours together, and they are now running – it seems endlessly – on Bravo! and TVOntario.

So many of the dancers I met while making the shows were impressive, but a few stood out even in that impressive company. Dame Ninette de Valois was ninety-eight years old and, once settled into her seat in front of the camera, she talked about Diaghilev with a clarity and passion that seemed incredible for someone her age. I could hardly believe I was sitting there talking to someone who had once actually danced for the great Russian impresario. Antoinette Sibley, for years a principal dancer in the company founded by Dame Ninette, the Royal Ballet, spoke with extraordinary eloquence and

Above left and right: In Moscow, with Vladmir Vasiliev and Uliana Lopatkina.
Below left: With Ekaterina Maximova.
Below right: On the road, with our cultural liaison officer (left) and
Neil Bregman in Tiananmen Square.

feeling, and did it so well that she needed no editing. My former partners Karen Kain and Evelyn Hart were equally eloquent. Kevin McKenzie, once a dancer with American Ballet Theater and now director of the company, impressed us all with his energy and humour. Fernando Bujones, another ABT star, showed up for the interview wearing a red jacket, black pants, and a black shirt, looking for all the world like a street hustler. All that was missing were the flashy rings. Then he sat down and surprised us all by proceeding to talk with great knowledge and insight on the history of dance. Fernando knew his dancers, his ballets, his dates, all about music – he turned out to be a great historian of his art. "To be a great Basilio in Don Q," he told us, "you have to have big *testicolos*" – which promptly got left on the cutting-room floor. Ghislaine Thesmar, of the Paris Opéra Ballet, was more fortunate with her comments on hormonal explosions and pregnancies. We left those in.

As I talked to some of the great dancers of our time, I was overwhelmed by the transient nature of what we do. It is not just that our careers are so short. It is that so little is left once they are over. Writers have their books, filmmakers and actors have their films, musicians their recordings, even stage actors can have tapes that seem to deliver more of what might have been present in their art than seems to be the case with dance. Dance films and tapes attempt to make performances live beyond the moment, but rarely do they seem to give anything but a shadow of what might have been experienced live. We were working with images of great performances, but for the most part they never moved me. Looking at some of the footage, I had a hard time understanding why it was that a dancer had been considered "great." In the end, I came to believe there was something antithetical about film and dance – that if it worked well as one, it didn't work as the other. Film demands close-ups, while dance demands that the whole body be viewed within context. Of all the films we used for the series, only a few seemed to capture the magic of performance, and it is hard to say what made the difference. The stand-out for me was *Romeo and Juliet,* danced by Margot Fonteyn and Rudolf Nureyev and directed by Paul Czinner. It was beautifully shot and edited. The dancers were always well framed, and the transitions to close-up were never disruptive of the dance. If anyone wonders what the magic was in the partnership of Margot Fonteyn and Rudolf Nureyev, they need only go to this thirty-year-old film. It may be just a shadow of what was present in the live performance, but there is definitely something there. The acting is totally natural, and the dancing sublime. I was moved to tears watching it, although I suspect that part of what makes it so moving is the realization that these two great artists are now gone. This celluloid is what we have to remember them by.

I learned a lot of history doing these shows. Odd fragments of information fascinated me. I found that underwear had its origins on the ballet stage. The pope, feeling that stage dancing was of dubious morality, decreed that all women dancers must wear underwear. That made me curious about the origins of the men's dance belt — which I can only assume arose as costumes got shorter and shorter, and it became necessary for men to wear more than simple underwear under their tights. Often the history had a personal resonance. Ballet had its origins as court entertainment — dancers were part of the court of Louis XIV at Versailles, providing entertainment for the king. I could relate to that. Over the years, I had done my share of entertaining kings and queens, princes and prime ministers. I had even performed at 24 Sussex Drive, when Mila Mulroney held a dinner to raise funds for Ottawa Ballet.

The show on the male dancer was naturally of particular interest to me. Ballet originated as a male art form, which was something I found a little harder to relate to, given that today it is so focussed on the ballerina. Listening to Anthony Dowell tell stories about never admitting to being a student at the Royal Ballet School for fear of the ridicule that would ensue, and Edward Villella talk about the fights he got into defending himself when the other boys in his neighbourhood found out he was a dance student – this all struck a chord. When Antoinette Sibley spoke so movingly about her lifelong partnership with Anthony Dowell, I kept thinking, "My God, why? Why did my partnership with Karen drift apart so early and why did theirs last for as long as they were dancers?"

It was comforting for me to hear these great dancers talk. Their concerns were my concerns, and, in a way, after doing the interviews, I felt less alone. We had similar judgements on what mattered in partnerships, what made a dancer great, what it meant to be musical. We might differ in our views of how a role should be interpreted, but even to engage in the discussion of how best to play Albrecht in *Giselle* gave me a sense that I had been part of a community. I came away with a sense of the finality of it all. Careers end. Those who had stopped dancing talked about that, too. The pleasures – and the pain – of giving up. I had a tendency to emphasize the positive; for years, while doing the series, and even for a short while after, I was in denial. I was actively denying that dance meant as much to me as it did. I would say to anyone who asked that it was great to be able to walk downstairs in the morning without being in pain. Slowly, I came to the realization that dancing meant far more to me than just a job, and that I was being flippant to avoid dealing with how I really felt, which was bereft.

I finally stopped dancing altogether at the age of forty-three. After *Footnotes*, Neil Bregman and I had signed a contract with the CBC to do another show. This was to be autobiographical, and George Anthony, the CBC executive who had commissioned the piece, stipulated that I should dance in it. I did not want to do this, but George was clear about what he wanted. If I didn't dance in it, he said, they wouldn't do the show, so reluctantly, I agreed. George thought it would be interesting to see the mature dancer alongside the young one. I knew this was a risky business – I could easily look bad – and was only prepared to do it with tailor-made choreography. René Daveluy, whose pieces work well for my movements, choreographed some solos for me, and we taped them. The day I looked at the unedited tapes of my performance was the day I stopped dancing forever. I looked choppy and stiff. My body was not moving with any fluidity at all. What was supposed to look effortless looked as though it had a great deal of effort behind it. At the time of the recording, my mind thought my body was doing it. It wasn't. I had trained four or five days a week for three months before the taping. It made no difference.

I no longer dance and I have come to terms with that. For a few years after I stopped, I could not bear to look at old tapes. My children went through a phase of watching the CBC tape of *La Fille Mal Gardée* a lot, and I would always walk out of the room. Now, I can look at these old tapes with a measure of distance. Not, I should hasten to add, that I look at them much at all – I haven't yet turned into Gloria Swanson in *Sunset Boulevard*. Dance has given me some great memories, and I have shifted from complaining that I can't do it any more to saying how wonderful it was when I could. It is a shift in attitude more than anything, but an important one, for it enables me to look back with a sense of joy rather than loss. If there is one thing I miss above all others, it is a sense of how good you feel when you give. There is a feeling of such well-being that comes from putting your heart and soul into something you love, and having all that effort appreciated. I was struck by something Evelyn Hart said in *Footnotes*. She talked about how, after an intense performance of *Romeo and Juliet*, she would go out into the night air, take a deep breath, and think how very lucky she was to be alive. I did that, too, Evelyn. If I miss anything about performing, it is that.

In truth, I did not give the ballet life up willingly. If I could have danced forever as well as I could when I was at my best, I would have. There is such joy in it, such total involvement of every part of your being. When you begin, with the blindness and arrogance of youth, you think that you can go on forever. I think of myself back then, wilfully ignoring all the things my father said to me when I was seventeen. The points he made have more resonance now, as I am struggling yet again to reinvent myself. I thought about them a lot when I went to visit him as he was dying.

He had fallen in the living room and broken his hip. That meant a hospital visit to get the hip replaced. After the operation, stubborn as always, he refused any kind of physio. He knew what was best, and that meant resting. The physiotherapists would try to get him up and walking, and, reluctantly, he would try a little, but his heart was not in it. There were many other problems – his bad heart, two strokes, failing eyesight, water retention – you name it. Any part of his body that could have problems, had them. He was eighty-seven.

My father was an old curmudgeon in that hospital, and not a very good patient. His inactivity, coupled with his state of mind, meant that he slowly withered away. It was nighttime, the last time I saw him – a frail man struggling, as he always did, for his life. Seconds would pass between each breath. As I sat and watched, I wished I could just hear his voice again. "Sit here, *mein* Peter, *mein* Frank. I have many stories to tell you." I may have dreaded his lectures but I loved his stories, those stories in which he somehow was always the hero, winning every fight, always finding ingenious ways by which to beat the enemy and survive. There were stories of regret, too. His weekends were always spent oil painting, and on the walls of the family home hangs testimony to a talent that was never allowed to grow into more than private space. My father and I had fought so hard, over so much – though nothing quite so much as my choice of career – that, by the end, we were strangers. Still, I sat there, wanting him to open his eyes one last time, to say goodbye. I left the hospital as the sun came up. I wasn't even there when he died at midday.

I am teaching now. I watch other young boys and men brimming full of the aspirations I once had. My son, Nicholas, I have to say, is not one of them. He is deeply suspicious of dancers, and to this day believes that all male dancers are gay, which in his view, and that of most of his friends, is not a good thing. I don't know where this comes from — it certainly isn't coming from home — but it is a deep-rooted and very common notion among many of his friends. I tell him not to be led by what his school friends say, although they are not all equally homophobic. Once, when his friend Ian was over, we were talking about our favourite music and sports figures. "In my field, dance," I started to say, and out of the corner of my eye I saw Nicholas flinch. I mentioned Erik Bruhn and Rudolf Nureyev, which seemed fine with Ian, but I could see Nicholas wanted me to stop talking. It was there in his eyes. *Stop talking, Dad. Stop talking right now.*

The stigma on male dancers has not disappeared. There are still jokes about men in tights, and people still laugh at them. It's better than it was, but dance is very far from being an equal-opportunity field, and we are a long, long way from the day when a male dancer has equal status with a ballerina. Nothing in the way we live supports this idea. If you want to be a great dancer, you must be prepared to show feeling — the softer feelings, as well as the more traditionally masculine ones of anger and rage. That's not something that men are ever encouraged to do, except perhaps in the kinds of men's movement groups that everyone laughs at. Add to this the fact that, to perform the classics of ballet well, the man must take a back seat for most of the show. He must do whatever needs to be done to allow the ballerina to shine. Again, taking the back seat to a woman is not something that our culture thinks of as being very masculine. To be a classical dancer, you must take pride in your body and be happy to display it, to welcome the gaze of the audience. Here, too, it is women, not men, who are taught to take pride in and to display their bodies, to allow the gaze of others to rest on them.

All this is changing – though slowly. In the almost thirty years since I first started to dance professionally, the dance world has changed along with the social world in which we live. Women have more choices in life and more social power than they had thirty years ago. Gay men are more accepted. Men are no longer quite the but-toned-down beings they once were, afraid to display emotion and afraid of women's power – but we have yet to see men valued for their feelings or for taking a back seat or for putting their bodies on display. So, to any young man who wants to be a dancer, I would first say, "Know this – and move on." You will live with it all your life, as you will live with people speculating about your sexuality. It doesn't matter. It isn't what dance is all about.

What matters is that you love to move and have a yearning to com-municate through movement. You have to love the physical labour of it all, because, make no mistake about it, dance is manual labour. Betty Oliphant once remarked that good dancers often come from working-class families; they are not afraid of hard physical work! All the time, there will be aches and pains, but what might be extremely painful for someone else becomes tolerable for dancers. You have to be able to work through pain, otherwise you won't get anywhere. Develop tunnel vision, but do so out of love for what you do, not as a way of avoiding the world. Enjoy the feeling of putting your feet into your tights and shoes, and feeling the floor beneath you. Enjoy the feeling of flying through the air, as it brushes against your body. Enjoy being able to communicate with an audience, and the whole sense of being intellec-tually, physically, and emotionally spent after a performance. Knowing that you did it well is an incredible feeling, and it can carry you for days. Dance, with its demand for total concentration, doesn't allow you to live in any time except the present. It is a wonderful way to live, because with every second, there is an awareness of time passing. You are squeezing every bit of experience from it. You are right there, in the moment, and there is nothing else. It helps if you like other dancers, as I did, for you will spend most of your time with them.

Learn to be persistent, to deal with discouragement, because it will happen on a daily basis. What I learned at a very young age was not to be discouraged by one thing that happened to go wrong that day while rehearsing, but to be persistent. Have patience. Believe that it will be better the next day. There will be many times when you work on something that worked perfectly well yesterday, only to find that today, nothing works. I remember coming in and being able to do beautiful double tours and landing them one after the other consistently, and then coming in the next day and not being able to do a single one. "Tomorrow is another day" – that was how I thought, and that was how I dealt with it. It may not have worked for everyone – definitely not for Karen – but for me, it did. I may have had to take two or three steps back in order to go forward, but I never let it get to me, because I knew that, if I let it get me down, it wouldn't be better tomorrow. It would be worse.

Know that, as Karen said in her autobiography, movement never lies. When you move, you show who you are and what you feel. You are completely exposed on stage. There is very little you can hide, and, if you are hiding, you show the audience you are hiding. Honesty is not just vital – it is the only thing that works. Movement must be motivated by honest emotion, and, if you don't have a sense of presenting movement because of that emotion, then it becomes just a series of steps, and only half of what the audience deserves. Always value the feeling, because in the end, it is what matters most.

In all this, know too that you cannot do it on your own. You will owe your success to many, many people. I would not have had a career in dance without a first dance teacher, Mrs. Morrison, who not only recognized my talent, but was also generous enough to pass me on at the right time to a teacher better equipped to give me what I needed. Betty Oliphant unfailingly expressed her belief in me, and, without her faith, I would not have made it. It wasn't just the confidence she gave me; it was also the sense that this was an endeavour of high seriousness. She viewed ballet as almost a religious vocation, and saw the stage as hallowed ground. In the face of such intensity, I felt commanded to take things seriously, too. Daniel Seillier gave me the sense that this was a career a man could have. It was enormously important to me to be taught by a man (after years of being taught by women) and to see, yes, men could dance, too. Daniel gave me strength and he gave me speed, and I needed every last ounce of both to get me through. Murray Kilgour and Nancy Schwenker, in their pas de deux classes, showed me not just technical movements but the spirit necessary for pas de deux — the openness, trust, and generosity that are vital for it to work. Rudolf Nureyev gave me both faith in myself and something like the purest perfection to strive for. Alexander Grant gave me the sense that I was an artist, and not just a working dancer who had to behave. He allowed me to grow up. The list could be expanded — to all the choreographers who gave me great roles to dance, and composers who gave me great music to dance to. If you are blessed with all these gifts, and on top of this are given the most valuable prize of all, a partnership, then you are doubly blessed. With Karen I had seven glorious years of a partnership that was priceless. I could ask for nothing more in a career.

My children will not follow in my footsteps. Neither have shown any interest in dance; they have sensibly gone their own way. Kyra, at fifteen, has great athletic ability and is on the school running team. Nicholas has another sport in mind. At the age of twelve, he has decided that he wants to learn boxing. It might not be my first choice for him, but we set out together to check out a place on Dundas Street that one of his friends recommended. As I walked into the gym, I felt I had walked into a scene from *Rocky*. A vast space, paint peeling off the

A recent photo of Erene and me with Kyra and Nicholas.

walls, and at the centre a boxing ring, surrounded by the numerous pieces of equipment that boxers need to take them through their paces. There was something slightly down-at-heel about it all. A few heavy-duty characters, muscle-bound and tattooed, were hanging around. A lone woman, who I later found out worked as a book-keeper at the gym, was in the ring, working out. I watched as Nicholas was taken through a training session lasting about an hour and a quarter. It surprised me, as I looked on, that there was much there I could identify with. There are elements of the process of training that remain the same regardless of physical discipline: I saw a series of exercises designed to develop balance, speed, reflexes, and endurance. These are all good qualities to have, and, though I have reservations about the boxing ring itself, the training seemed to encourage all the right things. At the end of the session, we were offered a special father-and-son rate, which I tactfully declined. Yes, I had done a little training myself, I offered, neglecting to mention at what – for which Nicholas was, I am sure, enormously grateful. He was elated after his session, and could not wait to get back at it. I am glad he has found something he enjoys. Clearly, the second male dancer in the Augustyn family will have to wait for another generation.

ACKNOWLEDGEMENTS

These are the memories I have of my world, both personal and professional. When I set out to tell my story, that of a Canadian male principal dancer, I knew it would be a difficult task. Little did I know, as I lunched with Avie Bennett at his favourite Chinese restaurant, just how difficult. I wish he had warned me.

Memoirs are flawed, and this book is no exception. Without the help of key individuals, this book would not have come as close as it is to the truth.

First and foremost, I would like to thank Barbara Sears for helping me tell my story. Her knowledge, expertise, and patience have helped me every step of the way. Remarkably, she has been able to put on the page the essence of my voice and manner, and intelligently map out my life in a cohesive form.

Pat Kennedy has been a generous and thoughtful editor, who removed many idiocies and prodded me to add insights. Copy editor

Lisan Jutras gave the manuscript the benefit of her meticulous eye.

I'd like to thank all the ballerinas I have danced with, especially those who have been instrumental in helping jog my memory – Karen Kain, Nadia Potts, Veronica Tennant, Vanessa Harwood, and Mary Jago.

Betty Oliphant, Celia Franca, Rudolf Nureyev, Alexander Grant, and Gert Reinholm were all central in the development of my life as an artist and a person. To them all, I express my gratitude.

To my brother, Peter, who I greatly admire, and to my parents, thank you for the values you passed on to me, and your love.

Thanks, too, to my ballet friends Linda Maybarduk, Tomas Schramek, Gloria Luoma, Debbie Gellman, Kathy Joyner, and Katherine Plaistowe for helping me whisk away the cobwebs of my past and for continuing to be devoted friends.

Three important professionals became my friends. Each, in their own way, helped guide my career – Michael Levine, Alex Dubé, and Victor Melnikoff.

Thanks to my academic teachers – Lucy Potts, Dawn Vale, Bruce Sittler, and Len Fawcett – and dance teachers, Eileen and June Morrison and Daniel Seillier, for their guidance early on in my life.

Thanks to Gordon Pearson and Ron Ward for their commitment and loyalty during the Ottawa Ballet days and their assistance in piecing together those years for this book. Also from the Ottawa Ballet days, Diana Kirkwood for her generous assistance. The Canada Council provided their assessors' reports on Ottawa Ballet. Douglas Byers provided a transcript of our CBC Radio program, "Personal Essay."

Thanks to James Neufeld for his excellent recounting of the National Ballet of Canada's history, *Power to Rise*, from which I drew valuable information. Ernest Hillen gave inspiration and solid advice. Sharon Vanderlinde, archivist at the National Ballet of Canada, patiently answered my questions, and was a great help with photographs. Others who helped with photographs: my mother, Elisabeth

Augustyn; Myra Armstrong; Neil Bregman; Samantha Cohen; Stephanie Hutchison; Marie Christine Mouis; Linda Maybarduk; William Reilly; and Kirstin Rydahl.

The book would not have been possible without the support of my loving family – my wife, Erene, and our two children, Kyra and Nicholas.

I apologize to all of you whose paths have crossed mine and are not named. Rest assured that you remain in my memory.

Frank Augustyn
Toronto, 2000.

PHOTO CREDITS

INDEX